# 40 DAY PRAYER GUIDES

# Praying for a Wayward Believer

### Powerful Day-by-Day Prayers Inviting God to Redirect Their Lives

# Eric Sprinkle and Laura Shaffer

*"Fanning the flame within"*

*40 Day Prayer Guides - Praying for a Wayward Believer, Powerful Day-by-Day Prayers Inviting God to Redirect their Lives*



All photos by Eric Sprinkle
Cover and interior design by Dave Fessenden

All text and images for this project were created by the authors of this book. In no part was AI used during the creation of this book, or its images.

ISBN: 978-1-7322694-9-1

Published by Adventure Experience Press in partnership with the fine folks at Honeycomb House Publishing LLC, Dave Fessenden, publisher and proprietor.

AdventureExperience.net

# Other Titles in the 40-Day Prayer Guide Series

## Praying for Godly Character

"Are you ready for a real adventure? Ignite your prayer life with this 40-Day guide and see what God will do!"

> | Award-winning author Amy Robnik Joob

## Praying a Blessing for Someone

Why waste your time worrying for a loved one, when you could spend that same time praying powerful prayers of salvation, breakthrough, and blessings instead? Join Eric Sprinkle and Laura Shaffer as they give you the blueprint for prayers that make a world of difference.

> | Linda Evans Shepherd, bestselling author of *Praying God's Promises* and *Praying Through Every Emotion*

## Praying for Someone's Salvation

Thoroughly comprehensive, practical, clear, inspiring and helpful. HIGHLY recommend.
Laura Shaffer along with Eric Sprinkle, has used her gentle, comprehensive and long-ranging experience of intercessory prayer to compose a guiding book which is user-friendly, encouraging and hope-inspiring. Hang on in there. Keep praying.

> | Early Amazon Reviewer

I like this book because the prayers are sooo much more powerful and give me ideas on what words to use through the day. See, I'm 8 1/2 and my friends at school do not know Jesus. This helps me focus.

> | Amazon Reviewer (with Mom)

I've been doing the 40 Day Prayer Guides — Praying for Someone's Salvation for about 2 weeks now and it's such a huge blessing. The prayers are wonderful, and working through each day's prayers has definitely been a blessing to me each morning. I am actively seeking time with the person I am praying for as a result of praying for him and we have had a lot of fun... plus it has laid a groundwork of trust for God to work in through our conversations.

> | Robin Shear, professional Joy Coach, author of the JOY BITES blog & an upcoming book about finding joy despite difficult circumstances. (www.joytotheworldcoaching.com)

# Praise for the 40 Day Prayer Guide series

You two make such a great team. Not only is Laura's content rich and practical, but Eric's photos also add a powerful and needed dimension to the prayers. Well done!

> Dick Bruso, Branding/Marketing Expert and Founder of "Heard Above The Noise"

You can pick up this book and begin praying immediately because the prayers are right there for you. Laura guides us as a "prayer warrior," sharing her words and letting us make them our own. Thanks to this book, applying prayer is easier than ever before."

> Laine Lawson Craft, best-selling author of *Enjoy Today Own Tomorrow*

I love the images and photos in these books. They are such an inspiration! Some of them excite me, others spark my imagination. And sometimes, one of them will completely transport me away to another place. A beautiful, quiet place, far away from life's stresses, where I can sit for a minute, reflecting on God's goodness, and on my wonderful prayer time with Him.

> Susan Neal, RN, MBA, MHA Director, Christian Indie Publishers Association, and best-selling author of *7 Steps to Get Off Sugar and Carbohydrates*

I loved this guide to pray blessings over others. Working through it not only blessed those I prayed over but also ended up blessing myself as well. Many of those I prayed for also ordered the book and began praying blessings for those in their lives.

What an impactful way to change the world (or at least the lives of our friends and families) through prayer.

> Kim Clinkenbeard, certified fitness coach for women over 40 and best-selling author of *Fitness. Food. Faith: Your Eternal "Why" for Everlasting Results* (www.getfitwithkimtoday.com)

# DEDICATIONS

### Eric

To the Recipient of my Kidney Donation, back on Dec 7th, 2022.
Whoever you are, wherever you are, I can't imagine looking at a clock
and watching it counting down your end of life, when suddenly, you
get a second chance! At everything. Just like we're praying for in this
book. I hope my little kidney is serving you well and you are attacking
life and living to the fullest with your new-found health and energy.

Also, to my Donor Buddy and lovely Co-author Laura —
We don't match blood types, so I couldn't give it to you, but I pray
that you're experiencing the same joy, healing and restoration
in your own life, following your recent transplant too :)

### Laura

To the "Wanderers" in my life who have made my heart tender to their journey.
Some have found their way back from their difficult path.
Some are still wandering.
Thank you for showing me how to offer prayers, forgiveness,
encouragement, and love in ways that I didn't see as important before.

Thank You Lord, for showing me that where there's breath, there's life.
And where there's life, there's hope.

And also, to my Amazing Hero Co-author Eric —
Who has enabled me to have a much more full and energetic life with a new
kidney, and offering me the encouragement and motivation to keep going.
May the Lord bless and keep you strong and healthy, Solo Kidney Partner!

# ACKNOWLEDGMENTS


- Many thanks to my amazing prayer partners over the years who have been a blessing in my life, teaching me how to pray by example through our Torah Group, Moms in Prayer groups, our Church Small Groups and Bible studies. Their prayers and encouragement are invaluable.

- Especially grateful thanks to those I've prayed with, sharing many prayers, many tears and many victories over the wanderers in our lives.

- As always, Eric thanks Panera Bread in Colorado Springs, North Las Vegas, and Tampa for a place to lay his laptop and work on writing, edits, and staying caffeinated.

- Last and always, to our Gracious Lord God, who not only directs our steps, but offers His grace and restoration whenever we wander off track, far beyond what we could ask or dare to imagine.

Soli Deo Gloria indeed.

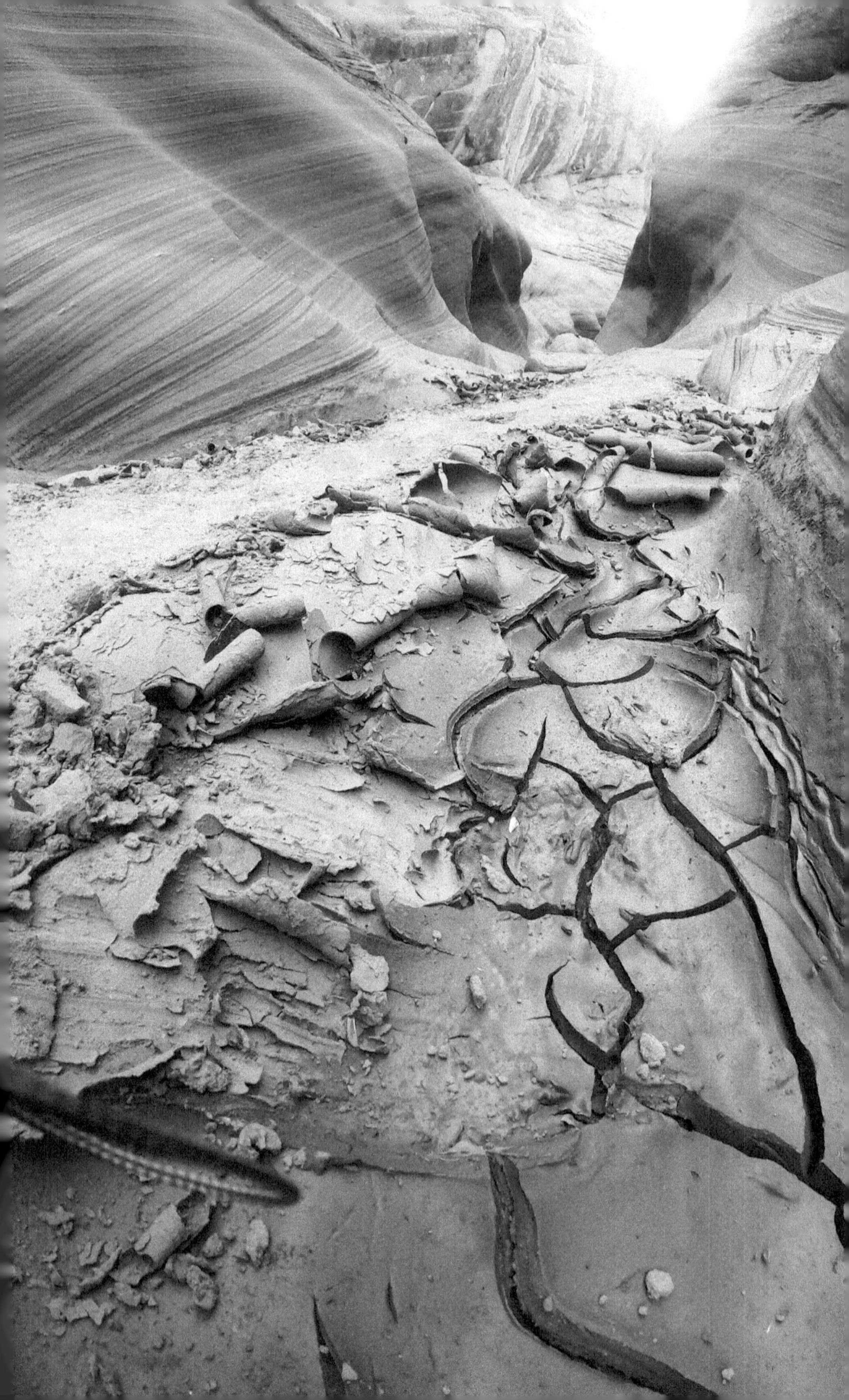

# INTRODUCTION TO THE 40 DAY GUIDES

**L**et's face it, our gracious Lord God has a thing for 40 days.

40 days of rain to flood the earth,

40 days spent in the wilderness before Jesus started his ministry,

40 days before the clock ran down on Nineveh to return to Him.

Over and over, we see 40 days as the time frame God uses for major changes in people and circumstances.

If I asked you to think of one person in your life, "a Wayward Believer who has wandered away from their faith", who immediately comes to mind? Have they ever come to mind before?

Is this the time to pray for their return to faith and living their life for God in a way you maybe never have before? Is it finally time for that someone to stop running, stop struggling, and just come home?

God loves it when we talk to and share with Him through prayer. Share our thoughts, our fears, our celebrations and concerns. The Bible tells us it's our prayers and petitions, with thanksgiving, that God uses to bring us peace, (Philippians 4:6-7).

Maybe it's just me, but I get the feeling that I've vastly underestimated just how powerful prayer can be...and maybe you've felt that way too?

So let's change it up. Let's make beautiful, Bible-based, laser-focused prayers a part of our daily routine for the next 40 days. Prayers for just one person. And instead of trying to think of the words, we'll use some of the most wonderful, powerful, stirring prayers you've ever heard, from our new mutual friend, Laura.

Let's read her prayers and make them our own. Let's read them silently or aloud, inserting the name of the person that came to mind. Don't worry, it'll be almost automatic by the time you get to Day 4.

What if we add a second person to pray for? What if we invite someone else to pray with us too? What if we invite a group of friends to join us on this 40 Day Prayer Journey? All lifting up the same person, plans and ideas to Him, asking together for the Almighty to change that person's life. To reveal Himself. To call them back to a deeper, richer life in Him.

Our Heavenly Father loves hearing our requests to Him through prayer. He loves blessing us with gifts too, often far more than we could ever ask or imagine.

I wonder what He wants to do in the life of that person who's wandered off?

I say we find out.

It's time to turn the page and begin a 40 Day Journey, focused on awakening and calling this person back to their Heavenly Father, who is waiting to celebrate the return of the person you've chosen. A journey that's most certainly going to impact them, and you as well.

Are you ready?

Let's do this.

# Introduction to Praying for a Wayward Believer

**D**o you have friends or loved ones who have wandered away from the Lord? For whatever reason have walked away from their faith?

You are not alone. Even God's children, Adam and Eve, and His chosen people, the Israelites, rebelled against Him. If you have children, or people you care about who have wandered from the Lord, there is hope.

Through praying for them, God can reveal Himself to You. And He will answer Your prayers. In His ways, and in His timing, He will use your 40 Days of prayers and the weekly reflections to show He has not abandoned you, or the ones you pray for.

Is there a son, a daughter, a friend who has simply strayed from living a life of godly, moral values, or even rejected their beliefs?

How could their life be different, better, if they returned to God?

Do you long to see them with their faith restored, on the path protected and directed by God?

I did.  I do.  Thinking of those in my life:

- Some have been hurt by the world and have been looking for a way to cover that pain, hurt, or disappointment.

- Some have been drawn away from their faith by temptations that took them father than they ever meant to stray, and kept them longer than they ever meant to stay.

- Some were led away by people, relationships they thought were good for them, but weren't, and they don't know how to break away from where they've been led.

- Some have grown numb and can't even remember who they really are, or what their life was like when they were walking with the Lord. They've lost their sense of identity and purpose in their search for something different.

I think of my Wayward Believers as living now with a forecast of "Cloudy with a chance of showers."

Cloudy because they are walking in a cloud — a haze of lies, misdirection and misinformation that comes from

- the world, the politics and philosophies of man,

- advertising and marketing slogans that suggest satisfaction of the flesh, wealth, and physical beauty are the determinants of success, and

- the temptations and lies of the evil one who has come to harm, kill and destroy.

But with a forecast of Showers of Blessing, because God is a loving God who created them and seeks still to have a personal relationship with them. And wants to bless them abundantly with His goodness and mercy, and draw them back into his flock, like sheep, to lead and care for them.

Are you willing to set aside a few minutes each day to pray for your loved one who has wandered away from their faith, to turn back to living a life for God?

We're going to ask the Lord to show them where they are and what they've been missing. To open their spiritual eyes and ears to their lives, and His truth about them. And to give them a renewed hunger and thirst for Him in their life.

# How to Use this 40 Day Prayer Guide

## Prayer Pages:

The guide will give you one daily theme with requests to pray for the 40 Days. If something interrupts your schedule, don't skip! Pick up the next prayer when you can.

These prayers are written to pray for the person you identify as someone who's a Wayward Believer, who's wandered away from the Lord. Just place their name in the blanks as you pray.

If you're praying for another person who isn't a Christian, consider also praying for their salvation. Our *40 Day Prayer Guide: Praying for Someone's Salvation* is also available. And see Appendix H (page 113) in this book if they seek you out asking how to be saved.

You can simply pray the prayer to yourself or out loud as it is, or you can let the Holy Spirit guide you and use your own words.

Or these prayers can be a springboard for your prayer time as the Holy Spirit brings more things to mind as you pray.

For instance, there may be times when a particular problem or situation will take precedence over a pre-planned agenda of prayer.

And there may be times when the Holy Spirit leads you to a different topic for blessing. Go for it.

Being flexible and sensitive to the Holy Spirit is the most important thing. Simply being intentional and consistent in your prayer time will help you be sensitive to the Holy Spirit.

## Reflection Pages:

Every 7 days the Guide will give you opportunities to:

- Write down your thoughts as you go along.
- Evaluate your progress.
- Look for ways God may be answering your prayers and thank Him.
- See how He is speaking to you personally about your prayer life, or how God might be leading you in your own life.

## Appendix Pages:

Check out our Appendix Section at the back of this book for valuable resources you might need during your 40 Day Journey or after. Whether it's how to Confess and Repent, put on Spiritual Armor before praying, or checking out how to Hear From God, we've got you covered.

## Before Beginning

We hope to encourage and accompany you on your 40 Day Prayer Journey with day-by-day prayers. We also understand that sometimes things get in the way that are unavoidable. If you have to miss a day, simply pick up where you left off. You don't want to miss out on a blessing or hearing from God.

In setting aside a few minutes each day to pray it may help to find a specific place or regular time of day to be intentional and consistent in your praying — like when you first get up, or while exercising, on your way to work or during a break from work, or in a room or seat in your home at a certain time, or at a natural break in your daily routine.

In preparing for prayer, two areas are important:

> 1 - **Confession and Repentance:** The Bible tells us in Psalm 66:18, *If I had cherished sin in my heart, the Lord would not have listened.* So it's important to ask God to search your heart and show you any sin you need to confess and repent of before you move into interceding for someone. See Appendix A (page 101).
>
> God has promised, *If we confess our sins, He is faithful and just and will forgive us our sins and purify us from all unrighteousness* (1 John 1:9).
>
> 2 - **Spiritual Armor for Battle:** Ephesians 6:10-11 tells us to be *Strong in the Lord and in His mighty power. Put on the full armor of God.* So we need to do that — name and pray on each piece before we pray for others. See Appendix B (page 102).

There are, of course, many things you can pray in asking for God's help in redirecting their lives. This is not meant to list or speak to all of them.

It will however, help you be more intentional and consistent in praying. And it is our hope, that by spending time in prayer, you will be open to the Spirit's leading. Learning to listen to the Holy Spirit guide you is most important.

It is our prayer that you will draw closer to God as you pray. That both you, and whoever you are praying for will benefit from the answers to your prayers.

And that you will be blessed as you *Lean in and Learn from the Lord* through prayer.

**A**re all prayers equal? It seems that God has listed some guidelines for us in Scripture that can either compromise or boost the effectiveness of our prayers.

There are even things that can cause Him to choose to step back or even disregard our prayers for a time. Yikes! Others are just the opposite, creating a multiplying effect on our prayers.

Have a look through and make sure nothing listed is going to get in your way over the next 40 Days. We don't want to be hindered in our prayers.

## Some Biblical Guidelines

♥ *The prayer of a righteous person is powerful and effective* (James 5:16).

Be sure you're following God and steering away from anything unrighteous or purposefully against God's ways for living. Holding grudges, being angry, indulging in wrongful thoughts or actions can all take away from the effectiveness of your 40 Day Journey.

♥ *The eyes of the Lord are on the righteous, and his ears are attentive to their cry* (Psalm 34:15).

We can rest assured we have God's complete attention when pursuing right living in our actions and choices.

♥ *But your iniquities have separated you from your God; your sins have hidden his face from you, so that he will not hear* (Isaiah 59:2).

Here we're told how to be sure nothing will get in the way of what we're asking. We need to confess our own sin when we pray. If we want to talk to God, let's clear out the background noise and use a strong signal with four bars.

♥ *Then Jesus told his disciples a parable to show them that they should always pray and not give up* (Luke 18:1).

No worries there, you're going to be praying for the next forty days, so you've got this!

♥ *When you ask you do not receive, because you ask with wrong motives, that you may spend what you get on your pleasures* (James 4:3).

Okay, so praying for a loved one to return for your own sense of pride or personal gain is not allowed, agreed?

♥ *This is the confidence we have in approaching God: that if we ask anything according to his will, he hears us* (1 John 5:14).

Let's all be sure we're asking for things in line with His will, His plans, His timing, and not our own. Trust that God is actively working to draw this person to Him, and bless them for His Glory, even if we're not seeing anything happening right away.

## Additional ideas that can boost the impact of your praying

- Pray these prayers out loud.
    *Does it help God hear them better? No. Does it help you? You bet! Praying out loud helps you slow down and focus on the person and words you're praying — allowing time for the Holy Spirit to meet you in your prayer. And that can make a difference all on its own.*

- As the Holy Spirit brings additional things to mind when you're praying, pray those too.
    *The Holy Spirit knows best what this person needs and what will bless them.*

- Pray the daily prayer multiple times a day.
    *When you eat? Morning and Evening? Or maybe whenever you start your car? When you think of the person you're praying for?*

- Pray for more than one person.
    *What happens if you say two people's names for each prayer?*

- Pray this 40 Day journey with a friend.
    *Both of you, lifting up the same person in prayer. Or each of you praying for your own someone but checking in with each other on your journeys.*

- Consider fasting at some point during the journey. See Appendix C (page 105).
    *Giving up TV, social media, or even certain foods for a week during your journey will only serve to sharpen your spiritual focus!*

## Listening

Prayer isn't just about talking to God. It's also about listening to what God has to say to you.

Some of these prayers will invite you to ask God to show you or teach you something. When you sense God showing or telling you something, it's important.

I encourage you to write what you're hearing in this book — in the margins, or the Reflection pages, or in the blank pages at the back, or in a notebook or journal of some kind.

God speaks in different ways. You probably won't hear an actual voice, like talking with another person. But you may have a strong sense in your spirit or your mind when something rings true to your situation.

Appendix D and E can help you understand how God might speak (pages 107 and 108).

Appendix F and G may help you understand if what you're hearing is from God (pages 110 and 112).

Write what you hear and check it with a pastor, counselor or trusted Christian friend.

# Table of Contents



### Help Them Remember Where They Were



### Prepare Them To See Where They Are



### Draw Them Back

## You Can Never Hide From His Love

Well you can't hide from His love or wander from His care

He is God Almighty and He is everywhere

When you have Jesus in your heart you never are alone

And you can never hide from His love


Sometimes we're tempted

Sometimes we fall

Sometimes we do the job halfway or not at all

But He just meets us where we are and loves us like before

'cause you can never hide from His love

Laura Shaffer © 1996

## My Commitment

Ephesians 3:14, 16, *For this reason I kneel before the Father...*
*I pray that out of his glorious riches he may strengthen you with power*
*through his Spirit in your inner being.*

In the Power of the Name of the Lord Jesus Christ, I am offering these prayers. Heavenly Father, I am trusting You to act and effect Your will during these next 40 days of prayer in _____'s life. Draw them back into a closer relationship with You so they will live their lives to honor You and bring You glory.

Father, I long to see _____ following Your ways and worshipping You as I have seen them do in the past. I hurt when _____ makes unwise decisions that cause them unnecessary pain and confusion.

I do not know all the forces that are currently influencing _____'s decisions and perspective. But the devil and the world and even their own flesh are at war with You and what is holy. Those forces seek to keep _____ away from You and the truth. And entice them into attitudes and behaviors that are harmful.

Especially during these 40 days of prayer, be their strength and spread Your protection over _____'s body, mind and spirit as only You can. Watch over their physical health so no illness sidelines them. Meet their emotional needs regarding their circumstances or where relationships have been broken by betrayal, unmet expectations or dishonesty. Heal any spiritual wounds caused by other believers, or where they have been believing lies that kept them away from Your perfect love, or desiring Your perfect will in their life.

Lord, *contend with those who contend with them and fight against those who fight against them* to give them victory over the enemies of their soul (Psalm 35:1).

I humbly ask for Your will to be done in and through _____'s life. Father, prepare them for Your message of love, encouragement, and direction. Make them aware every day that they need You. Remind them of Your unconditional love, and that You are with them, always. Amen.

# Help Them Remember Where They Were

## Return the Joy of Their Salvation

Psalm 51:12, *Restore to me the joy of your salvation, and grant me a willing spirit, to sustain me.*

Heavenly Father, _______ has been away from Your influence for a while, choosing to live life in the world, with the world's values and influences. It has taken them away from the life I believe You wanted for them. And it breaks my heart.

They've been missing out on the guidance You would give and the blessings that come with that. Missing the opportunities to live out the purpose You planned for them and use the gifts and talents You placed in them. And missing the wisdom You would impart that would help _______ make wise decisions and better choices.

Let this be a time of renewed spiritual awareness, growth, and renewal for _______. Help _______ remember who You are, the relationship they had with You, and how You were involved with and worked in their life. Give _______ a renewed hunger and thirst to know You that way again.

Father, renew that sense of Your presence with them that will be an awesome sense of accountability, and an amazing sense of reassurance of Your protection.

Remind _______ what led them to You in the first place. And help them recall the joy they felt when they let go of all the burden of their sin, and were washed clean. Let them remember the joy of praying to You and receiving Your blessings in their life. Give _______ the desire to know those joys again. And show them the path that will return them to the joy of their salvation. Amen.

**Recall Scripture**

Isaiah 55:8, 11, ...*declares the* L*ord*...*so is my word that goes out from my mouth: it will not return to me empty, but will accomplish what I desire and achieve the purpose for which I sent it.*

**H**eavenly Father, recall Your Word, bring scripture to _______'s mind. Let the memories of hearing and understanding and knowing Your word fill their thoughts. Help _______ apply the meaning of those words to their life now.

Bring to mind Bible stories, lessons, songs that tell Your truth, and allow those to create a longing in their heart for those times of knowing You. Let verses they've memorized echo in their intellect. Let melodies and lyrics float into _______'s memory so the truth of those songs seeps into their consciousness, becoming something they hum or sing, suddenly aware of the meaning and truth of what they used to hold dear.

It could be something as simple as a children's song like "Jesus Loves Me" that would stir feelings of Your love and acceptance. Or Bible stories they heard as a child that tell of Your love, provision, protection, sovereignty or power that reminds them how much they need that in their life now. It could be a scripture-based sermon _______ heard somewhere in their past that made an impact on them at the time, and they realize now, what they're missing from their life. Or a single line of scripture that calls to them with just what they need to hear.

Father, let none of these stories, songs or scriptures return void, but accomplish what You, Lord, desire in them — a Wayward Believer returning to You. Amen.

## Renew a Sense of God's Presence/Power

Isaiah 41:10, *So do not fear, for I am with you; do not be dismayed, for I am your God. I will strengthen you and help you; I will uphold you with my righteous right hand.*

Heavenly Father, there is no place _____ can go that You are not there with them.

Help _____ sense Your presence with them in real and tangible ways that they notice and can experience. Let it be an awesome sense of accountability as well as bring amazing comfort. Give _____ a peace they haven't felt in a while. Don't let them fear Your presence, but embrace it as a warm blanket of security and protection.

Father, Your presence with _____ is a gift that can change their sense of reality. Walk and talk with them to bring them to an awareness of Your ability to hear their worries, fears, dreams, and Your willingness to tackle those with Your power. Let Your presence show how things can be different as they draw near to You again.

Father, Your power is ultimate and greater than any other above or below the earth. You are the Maker of all things. King over all the earth, reigning Sovereign and Supreme — God of Angel armies!

You are forever _____'s Creator and Savior. And no one and no thing can stand against You. No power, ruler, or authority. Nothing in heaven, on the earth or below it. Your power can span any distance, overcome any obstacle, move any object, overpower any influence.

So Father, be at work in _____'s life overcoming whatever influences have brought them to the place they are now. Let _____ see Your power at work releasing them from whatever has captured their attention and hearts and led them away from You. Let _____ feel Your power working for them in a way that opens their eyes and blesses them.

Father, let _____ see and recognize Your presence and Your power with them in a way they haven't experienced in a while. Let them be drawn to it. And to You. Amen.

## Recall They Are Loved

Romans 8:38–39, *For I am convinced that neither death nor life, neither angels nor demons, neither the present nor the future, nor any powers, neither height nor depth, nor anything else in all creation, will be able to separate us from the love of God that is in Christ Jesus our Lord.*

Heavenly Father, You have promised that nothing can separate _____ from Your love for them. I declare that You have poured Your limitless, sacrificial love over _____! And remind both of us there is nothing that will remove that love from them! Nothing they have ever done or can ever do, will keep You from loving them.

If _____ has forgotten how it feels to be loved like that, they may even feel totally unlovable. Or feel they can never earn their way back into Your acceptance.

Thank You that Your love is not based on what _____ can do to earn it. They don't have to work for it, or even deserve it. You will always love _____, because Your love is based on *who You are!* Your character and Your promise. And You love _____ unconditionally!

Despite any shortcomings, mistakes, failures, or even willful disobedience, You love _____. You already know about every past, present, and future sin, and still love _____. Beyond how any human can love, Your love is infinite, unfailing, perfect, rich in mercy, always forgiving, sacrificial; it casts out fear, and is permanent.

Father, help _____ understand Your love: how wide and long and high and deep it is for them personally. More than just reading about it, help _____ really know it, in their heart and in their spirit, not just in their head.

Father, I proclaim that love, Your love over _____. Open their heart to accept it. And let it win them back to You. Amen.

## Remember Their True Identity

Psalm 139: 13-14, *For you created my inmost being; you knit me together in my mother's womb. I praise you because I am fearfully and wonderfully made; your works are wonderful...*

Heavenly Father, I declare that You are _______'s Creator! You knew them before they were born, and You created them intentionally and purposefully. You designed and gave _______ the body, mind and spirit You planned for them to have. You gifted _______ with talents, skills, knowledge, personality, and spiritual gifts deliberately.

Show _______ their true identity, made in Your image. Do not let them define themself by a job or a role that carries responsibilities and expectations that determine their self-worth based on how well they perform. And do not let the world or current social values determine _______'s thinking or feelings about who they could or should be.

Rather than being dissatisfied with how they look or the talents they have or don't have and seeking value in the world's eyes, let _______ begin to see themselves through Your eyes, from Your perspective. And let that be the source of their sense of true identity, value and worth.

Father, empower _______ with a fresh revelation that they are created in your image, on purpose — to be who they are. And that everything about them is a gift from You. Open their eyes to see that truth. That all they have is from You. That it is good. And that everything they see around them is Your Creation as well.

Show _______ how to believe and behave according to their God-given identity. And be able to acknowledge You as their Creator. Amen.

## Free from Condemnation

Romans 8:1, ***Therefore, there is now no condemnation for those who are
in Christ Jesus.***

Heavenly Father, thank You for removing condemnation from _____. And for
being a God of many chances. Remind _____ that none of us are judged
by our greatest shame or worst mistake. Jonah disobeyed and ran in the
opposite direction. But You brought him back and many were saved when he
returned to You and was obedient to Your call.

Rather than condemnation, which the evil one uses to ensnare and drag them
down, _____ is already freed from the defeat, guilt, shame and hopelessness of
that.

You offer conviction — a firmly held value or opinion, something to stand
up for and believe in. Conviction that comes from You lifts us up and can inspire
_____ to do better, to be better. It can motivate and empower _____ to think and
behave in a new, different way, and to return to what they believed before.

Thank You that no matter how far _____ has wandered, You stand with open
arms to embrace, welcome, and bless them anew. Help _____ look beyond their
past, and move forward into all that You have for them now.

Thank You that Your mercy is new every morning, and for going after _____,
pursuing them, and offering new chances. Show them new ways to think, to act,
to speak. Help them make the most of the opportunities You bring. And in that
freedom, be drawn back to You. Amen.

# *Reflections*

You are not alone. Even God's children, Adam and Eve, and His chosen people, the Israelites, rebelled against Him. If you have children, or people you care about who have wandered from the Lord, there is hope.

Through these circumstances, God can reveal Himself to You. And He will answer Your prayers. In His ways, and in His timing, He will use your 40 days of prayers and the weekly reflections to show He has not abandoned you, or the ones you pray for.

If you have been able to be consistent in praying this week — good for you!

If not, what has gotten in your way? And how can you remedy that?

_______________________________________________________

If you have missed any days, begin now from the last day you prayed.

In your prayer time this week, has God shown you anything about Himself? About the one you're praying for? About yourself?

_______________________________________________________

_______________________________________________________

Thinking back over the prayers you prayed this week…

Do you remember when you accepted Jesus' free gift of salvation? Could you tell someone about that? It's part of your own testimony. Write about that here. And ask God to renew your sense of joy in your salvation and your eternal life with Him.

_______________________________________________________

_______________________________________________________

_______________________________________________________

How have you sensed God's presence and power in your life? Write some of those ways here, and share with someone, asking how they sense it.

_______________________________________________________

_______________________________________________________

_______________________________________________________

Are you aware of Who You Are in Christ? Your true identity? What is true of you is also true of the Wayward Believer you're praying for. Check out Appendix I (page 114) in the back of the book.

Put your own name in the Scriptures and say them out loud as an encouragement for yourself. Consider adding one to some of your prayers with your Wayward Believer's name in it.

Write a few here that you like:

_______________________________________________

_______________________________________________

_______________________________________________

Write a few words describing how you see your loved one - where they are now, how they're living their life, decisions they've made.

_______________________________________________

_______________________________________________

Write a few words of how you feel about that:

_______________________________________________

_______________________________________________

In prayer, give what you see and the feelings you have about them over to God. Write it here if you want.

_______________________________________________

_______________________________________________

Now ask Him to help you:

- Forgive _______ for wandering away.
- Forgive their friends or influences that may have drawn them there.
- Forgive yourself and remove any guilt you may feel you have contributed.
- And to forgive Him, God for allowing them to wander away.

I believe where there is breath, there is life. And where there is life, there is hope, "… *and hope does not disappoint, because the love of God has been poured out within our hearts through the Holy Spirit who was given to us*" (Romans 5:5 NASB).

Sit for a moment and imagine what your loved one would look like, behave like when they turn back to God. Write a few words that would describe them then.

_______________________________________________

_______________________________________________

Ask God to keep that picture of hope alive as you pray for your loved one. And trust that His love, plans, purpose, protection, provision and power can and will overcome whatever darkness is at work in your loved one's life.

# **P**repare Them to See Where They Are

## No Victim Mentality

Deuteronomy 20:4, *For the Lord your God is the one who goes with you to fight for you against your enemies to give you victory.*

Luke 10:19, *I have given you authority...to overcome all the power of the enemy; nothing will harm you.*

Heavenly Father, help _____ lay down their victim mentality. At some point, either because of the evil and abuse of other people or refusing to accept responsibility for their own actions, they may have chosen this. It has robbed them of their ability to make wise decisions and take charge of their life.

Living as a victim has brought some benefit that has won them attention from others. It allows _____ to complain, rebel, blame others, wallow in self-pity, and feel helpless. It prevents them from being accountable for their own actions, and for taking responsibility for their own life. That puts them in a hopeless, powerless frame of mind.

It is not worth the cost and will ultimately blind _____ to see their need for a savior and receive the love and help You offer. And will keep them in a kind of captivity that freezes them in place instead of moving forward with their life.

Lord, help _____ be an overcomer! To accept Your love empowering them to pray, accept Your power to work in their life, and move forward in their faith no matter their circumstances or past mistakes. Amen.

**Expose the Lies**

*2 Corinthians 11:3, But I am afraid that just as Eve was deceived by the serpent's cunning, your minds may somehow be led astray from your sincere and pure devotion to Christ.*

Heavenly Father, show _____ where they have believed a lie and were misled into making unwise decisions. Even where the lies were disguised by a twisted little bit of truth, rip off the blinders that have kept _____ living under the influence of deception, misdirection and falsehood.

Help them see the damage to their life, their future and their values by believing and acting on these lies. And how they have been led away from You. Strengthen _____'s desire not to be lied to anymore. Let them see Your truth: about what is right and wrong. About what is good and evil. About what is best for them and their future.

Even small lies and deceptions can pull _____ away from You so teach them how to listen for You, and guard their mind. Reveal any traps that are hidden. And the hook buried beneath the lure and temptation of words used by the world, the flesh and the evil one.

Lord, it's bad enough these lies have affected _____'s behavior, relationships, and beliefs about the world, but expose any lies they've been led to believe about You or their faith. It's easy to mislead someone when you isolate them with lies.

_____ may believe that You don't love them anymore. That they've fallen too far or made too many mistakes to ever be forgiven and accepted.

Father, crush those lies! Show _____ that You never left them - You are right there beside them now. And they only need to turn to You - call out Your name - and You will answer and greet them with loving arms. Let _____ see that You never moved, never turned Your back on them, and are waiting for them with open arms. Amen.

**Evaluate Influences**

1 Kings 3:9, *So give your servant a discerning heart...to distinguish between right and wrong.*

Heavenly Father, help _____ look around with clear vision and give them the wisdom needed to recognize the negative influences that led them to where they are now, and the positive influences they ignored when they should have paid attention. Help them understand why they believed those lies that took them away from You or trusted those sources in the first place.

Show _____ where the places they went, or people they spent time with, led them away from Your wisdom. And how they can change their schedules or activities to minimize or avoid those people and places now. Show them how make better choices with their time, their money, their energy, their relationships, starting now.

Help _____ also see the good habits they have and how those can get them back to where they need to be in living a godly life again. Show them which relationships are good for them and play an honorable role in their life. Reveal those positive influences in how they spend their time, energy, and money. And bring it to their attention if they get out of balance and drift back toward any of those negative influences.

Thank You that You promise wisdom when _____ asks for it. Father, help _____ seek it now. Amen.

OBJECTS IN MIRROR ARE
CLOSER THAN THEY APPEAR

## Idolatry

1 Samuel 12:20-21, ***Do not be afraid...do not turn away from the Lᴏʀᴅ, but serve the Lᴏʀᴅ with all your heart. Do not turn away after useless idols. They can do you no good, nor can they rescue you, because they are useless.***

Heavenly Father, if ______ has embraced idolatry or the traditions of some other form of religion, show them how to step away from that. Do not let them become so enthralled with any idea, organization, or false god that they bow down and sacrifice their time, energy, money, or talent to it. Protect them as they turn away from false religions and idols.

Teach ______ how to remove any idolatrous items from their homes. Anything from wood or stone idols, to things that may look like innocent entertainment, can expose them to evil or witchcraft - like tarot cards, Ouija boards, horoscopes, fortune telling, channeling, seances, or those who claim to speak to the dead or summon the devil. These pose a spiritual risk of drawing them back into ungodly worship. Lead ______ to also eliminate ungodly traditions or behaviors from their schedule.

Money, fame, power, even some good things can become idols if they become the focus of someone's life and draw them away from worshipping You, the One True God.

Give ______ new ways to honor and worship You that will replace those ways of idolatry.

Show them the false and damaging effects of those ungodly practices. Remove the fear and anxiety they have in facing the world. That all comes from facing a world without You.

Reveal the truth and blessing that comes from worshipping You. Let them sense the strength You give them to move forward in faith, sensing and understanding that they are not alone, and never were. Amen.

**Abundant Life**

John 10:10, *The thief comes only to steal and kill and destroy; I have come that they may have life, and have it to the full.*

**H**eavenly Father, You have come to give life abundantly. So no matter where _______ is - geographically, physically, situationally, emotionally, financially, spiritually - no matter what kind of problem they are dealing with, do not let _______ ever entertain or be seduced by the idea that suicide, or self-harm is the answer or even an option to their problems. Do not let them entertain thoughts of suicide or make a plan to take their life.

Overcome, and reveal the source of any lies or deceitful thoughts that have been allowed into _______'s mind or heart. Open their eyes to the truth that they need You in their life again. Place people around _______ right now who will be witnesses to the hope and the truth that is in You. Break through whatever is keeping them in dark moods or downcast emotional states. And allow _______ to once again feel the love You have for them.

As You have unlimited power, Lord, You can do immeasurably more than I can ask or imagine. Intervene, in the plans of the evil one who comes to harm, kill, and destroy. Guard _______'s life. Breathe Your love and encouragement into them now to deliver _______ from any darkness that seeks to overwhelm or destroy them.

Father, fight for _______'s very life! Defeat the work of the evil one. Pour out Your Holy Spirit on _______ to be empowered to reject the influences of evil. Open their eyes to see that You have not left them. And that You stand with them to live the abundant life You came to give them. Amen.

_______________________________

*If you see or sense emotional stress, or they express feeling hopeless, no reason to live, or talk about self-harm call or text 988 24/7/365 or go to 988lifeline.org for help with a counselor.*

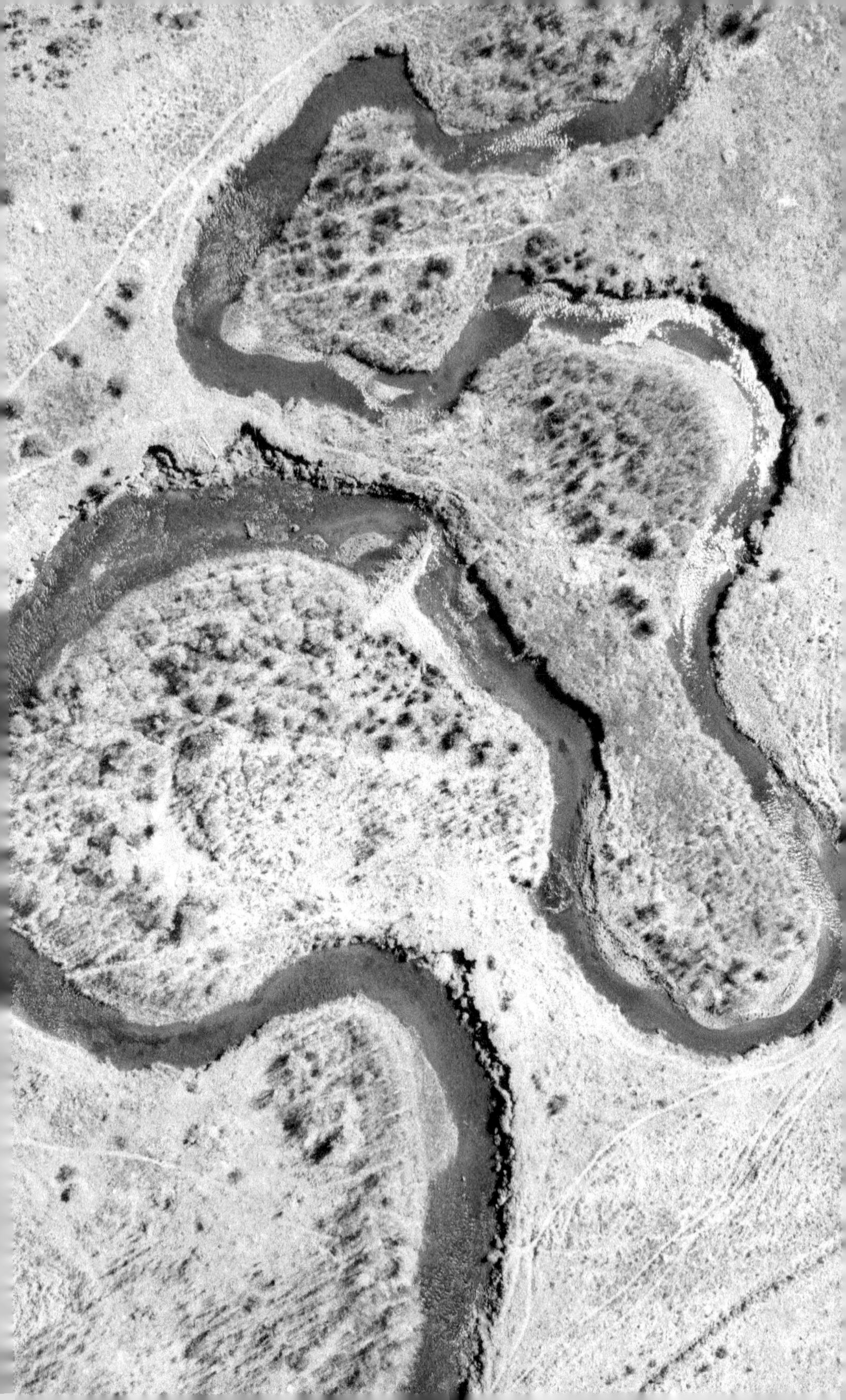

**Waywardness**

Hosea 14:4-6,
> *I will heal their waywardness*
> *and love them freely,*
> *for my anger has turned away from them.*
> *I will be like the dew to Israel;*
> *he will blossom like a lily.*
> *Like a cedar of Lebanon*
> *he will send down his roots;*
> *his young shoots will grow.*
> *His splendor will be like an olive tree,*
> *his fragrance like a cedar of Lebanon.*

Heavenly Father, show ______ that even in their waywardness, You are still there with them. You stand ready to heal them through Your love, and have turned Your anger away from them.

Help ______ realize that with Your help they can blossom again, coming back into the joy of using the talents and spiritual gifts You've already given them. And rather than being like a bush in the dry desert that is barely alive, that they can be tall and straight and strong, like a cedar of Lebanon.

Teach ______ how to be rooted again in You; like a cedar, drawing strength from time spent in prayer with You. And see new growth in their life from reading and living by Your Word, the Bible. Let them marvel again at Your amazing Creation!

And like an olive tree that grows in community with roots, trunks, and branches intertwined with other olive trees, show ______ how they will thrive again in a community of believers - being nourished and supported even in hard times. Lead them to such a community.

Father, make ______ like an olive tree that can stand and be fruitful once again. Amen.

## Wake-up Call

Ephesians 5:14-15, ...*"Wake up sleeper, rise from the dead, and Christ will shine on you." Be very careful then, how you live — not as unwise but as wise.*

Heavenly Father, would You open _____'s physical and spiritual eyes and give them clear vision to see what's going on around them. Let them view their circumstances from Your perspective.

Give _____ a wake-up call to realize where they are in their life in relation to where You are. Get their attention in a dramatic way, to show them how far they've drifted and pulled away from all that You have for them.

Help _____ remember what their life used to be - the values they had that governed their decisions. Remind _____ what living a godly life looks like. Place people around them who will be positive and encouraging examples and influences. Help them truthfully evaluate where they are and what the path back to You would look like.

Show _____ how to examine their thoughts, their activities, their behavior, their decisions, their work, their entertainment, their relationships to see what took them so far from You. Help them see if the places they go, or the people they see, or how they spend their money or time have taken them off Your path. And how to evaluate what is needed to get them back on a righteous path.

Point _____ to the first step they can take that will lead them back in Your direction. And reward even the baby steps they take toward You. Amen.

# Reflections

If you have been able to be consistent in praying this week — good for you!
If anything has gotten in your way, how can you remedy that?

_______________________________________________________________________

In your prayer time this week, has God shown you anything about Himself?
About the one you're praying for? About yourself?

_______________________________________________________________________

_______________________________________________________________________

Thinking back over the prayers you prayed this week...
Not giving in to Victim mentality, and recognizing lies someone has believed
are challenges everyone faces. Ask God if there are things You need Him to
expose in your own life. List anything He shows you.

_______________________________________________________________________

_______________________________________________________________________

_______________________________________________________________________

It can be hard to recognize when something is a negative influence in your life.
And even harder to avoid or cut it out of your life. Write if you've experienced that.

_______________________________________________________________________

_______________________________________________________________________

_______________________________________________________________________

Do you sense any ungodly influences in _______'s life? It's so easy to let things
or desires take priority over God. Anything that requires more and more time and
energy, money and talent can be an idol. And some things can lead to real darkness.
Rather than mentioning those things, list them here and pray over them
specifically.

_______________________________________________________________________

_______________________________________________________________________

_______________________________________________________________________

- If you sense occult influences in their life, put on the Spiritual Armor before
  you pray. See Appendix B (page 102) and add a sentence to every prayer
  for God to open their eyes and convict them to remove those influences
  from their home and life.

- If you see or sense emotional stress, or they express feeling hopeless, no reason to live, or talk about self-harm call or text **988 24/7/365** or go to **988lifeline.org** for help with a counselor.

If you know of a community of believers or a place or opportunity _______ could connect with positive, godly influences, consider letting them know about a gathering or inviting them to go with you. Note any upcoming opportunities they might consider.

Is there a time You received a Wake-Up Call? Write about it.

_______________________________________________________________

_______________________________________________________________

_______________________________________________________________

Have you shared that with anyone? What was their reaction?

_______________________________________________________________

_______________________________________________________________

Is there someone you can share it with now?

You may be able to see things you want to fix in the life of the one you're praying for. Bring those to God, and ask God to help you be willing to give Him control of _______'s life, decisions, influences. That may mean holding your tongue when you want to offer your opinion.

Here's a prayer for you:

*Father, I pray that I would be a tool in Your hand for godly purposes. Use me to accomplish Your will. And never let me forget that Yours is the strength and the wisdom by which anything is accomplished with the people I love.*
*Help me show Your grace and mercy and compassion to them.*
*When asked, help me give wise and godly advice, not just my own preferences. Let my words be instructive and gentle, and line up with Your truth, spoken in love for the benefit of the wanderer. And hold my tongue when the words come from some other motivation.*
*Help me spread Your peace in their life when it would be easier to spread my own brand of how things should be. Help me let go of my own expectations of them, freeing them up to know the fulfillment of Your plans and purposes.*
*Help me be patient with Your timeline for their development and maturity. And be consistent to pray for them to be empowered and guided by the influence of Your Word, and what You speak to them and through godly mentors and circumstances.*
*Let me draw strength from You. Let me be guided by You. And let me rest in Your strong and skillful hands, remembering: The power is not in the tool, but in the one who wields it. Amen.*

# **D**raw Them Back

**Dreams and Visions**

Joel 2:28, *I will pour out my Spirit on all people. Your sons and daughters will prophesy, your old men will dream dreams, your young men will see visions.*

Heavenly Father, You are at work at all times and in every place around the world, and in the life of every person. Even those people without a translation of the Bible have access to You as You reach them with dreams and visions of who You are. And of Your love for them.

Please give _______ a dream or vision. Whether it's a dream or vision of future events, or a revelation of the power that You possess as Creator of this universe, reach their mind and heart and spirit. Communicate Your truth that even as Almighty God, You love _______ and desire to have a closer, personal relationship with them.

Some around the word have had dreams while they slept, where You revealed Yourself as Savior. And waking up, the truth remained with them. Others have had dreams about their life and woke up with the realization that they needed a change: You in their life! Father, give _______ a dream, and wake them up with a realization of who You are.

Still others have had experiences that caused them to have a flash or a waking vision that figuratively woke them up to the reality that they had been living their life focused on the wrong goals. And they were then drawn back to You. Father, get _______'s attention with an experience or revelation they can't deny.

Lord God, You can bring this kind of change in _______. Reach them in a way that I cannot. In a way that only You can, change the course of their life, renew their faith, by drawing them back to You. Amen.

## Spiritual Protection

Psalm 121:3–4, *He will not let your foot slip – he who watches over you will not slumber; indeed, he...will neither slumber nor sleep.*

Heavenly Father, as _______ is Your child, You have promised to watch over and protect them. Let them see by experience that You are there - even in the challenges and painful lessons in life.

I pray these Psalms over _______ now as statements of Your protection over all aspects of their life, health, marriage, family, relationships, home-school-work, finances, mental, emotional and spiritual well-being and growth:

Psalm 35, *Contend, Lord, with those who contend with _______. Fight against those who fight against _______. Take up shield and armor; arise and come to their aid. Brandish spear and javelin against those who pursue them. Say to _______, "I am your salvation."*

*May those who seek _______'s life be disgraced and put to shame; may those who plot _______'s ruin be turned back in dismay. May [the enemy] be like chaff before the wind, with the angel of the Lord driving them away; may their path be dark and slippery with the angel of the Lord pursuing them.*

*Psalm 91, Surely he will save _______ from the fowler's snare and from the deadly pestilence. He will cover _______ with his feathers, and under his wings they will find refuge; his faithfulness will be _______'s shield and rampart. Amen.*

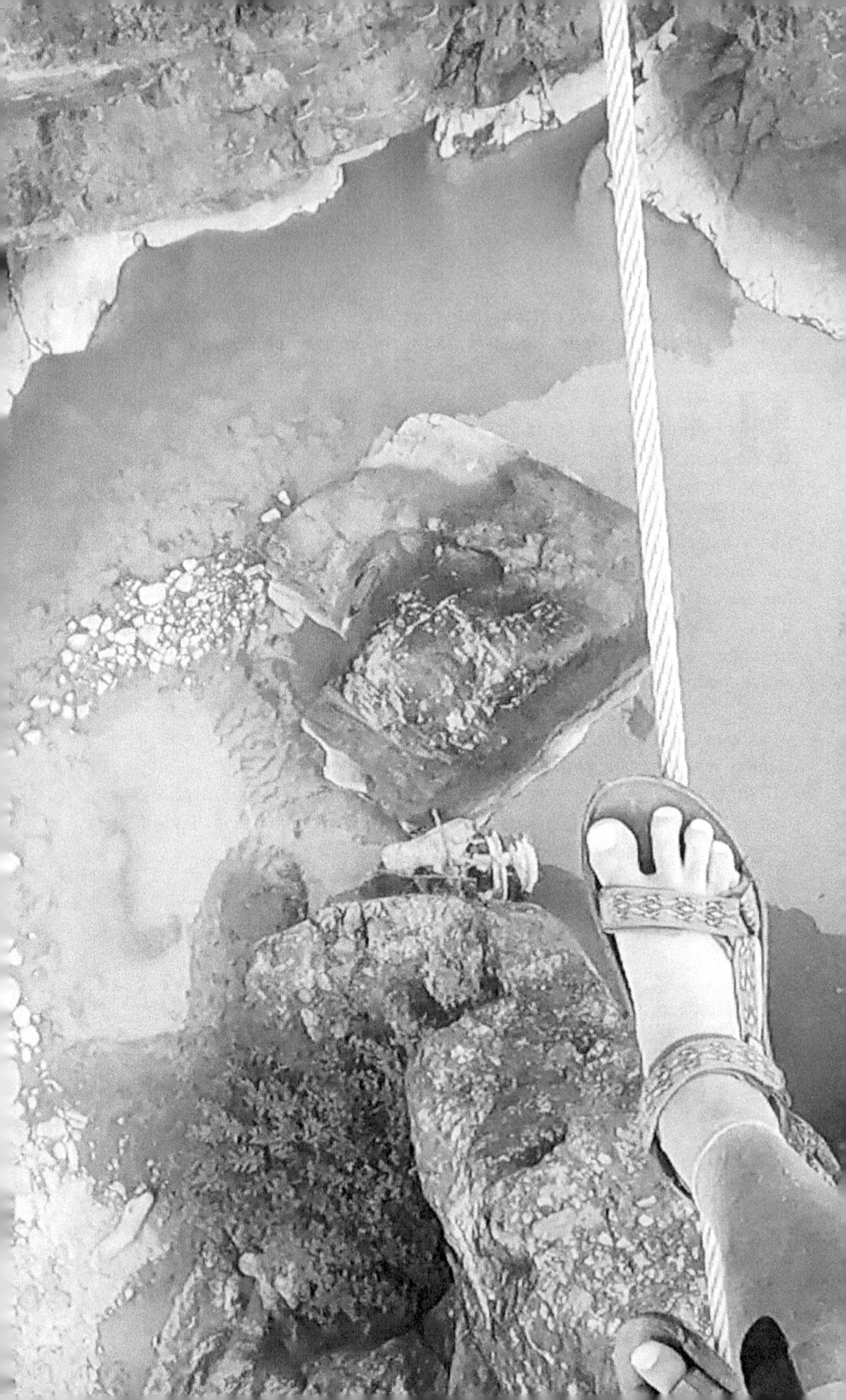

## Use Challenges and Trials

**2 Peter 2:9, *...the Lord knows how to rescue the godly from trials...***

Heavenly Father, use every circumstance in _____'s life to call them back to You. Rather than just reacting to what's going on in their life, let challenges and even negative experiences be teaching opportunities for them to see You at work.

Often, it's something unpleasant that turns people to You. So let every challenge or trial in _____'s life not be wasted, but cause them to look deeper and see a spiritual meaning. And in hardship, to call out to You. Make that a powerful opportunity to reach and teach them.

Help _____ grow in areas where they need to develop strength or wisdom. And even when they face fear, and see no way out, expand their perspective!

Deliver them in wonderful and unexpected ways so they learn about Your provision, Your care, Your love. Showing them how You can make a way where there seems to be no other way.

Open _____'s spiritual, eyes and ears to the blessings You give them even in hard times: wisdom, strength, endurance, guidance, energy, insight, encouragement.

Lord, there is nothing too big or too small for You to overcome to reach _____. Use even their trials and challenges to reveal Yourself to _____. Amen.

## Heal Past Hurts

Jeremiah 30:17, ***"But I will restore you to health and heal your wounds,"** **declares the LORD...***

Heavenly Father, I know ______ has been through painful circumstances that have hurt them. Whether caused by accident, misunderstanding, rejection, betrayal, the evil one, or some forgotten incident, tear down the wall ______ has built up between You and them. Dissolve any bitterness and heal the hurt that remains; physically, emotionally, mentally, or spiritually.

Show them how those hurts have led them away from You, the One who could heal them and resolve those issues. Encourage them with someone who can provide wise counsel and support during this vulnerable time. Someone who can check their attitudes and guide them in making godly decisions.

Send angels to provide a hedge before them and behind, along their sides and above and below to protect ______ from further hurt while You are healing them.

Give ______ faith to trust what You say: that You love them and that Your love is greater than whatever difficulty they're going through. Thank You for being their Jehovah Rapha, their Healer. It may take time, but begin the healing process so ______ can see Your Light through whatever darkness they've been facing. Amen.

## See God's Blessings

James 1:17, *Every good and perfect gift is from above, coming down from the Father of heavenly lights...*

Heavenly Father, open up Your storehouse and pour out such blessings on _____ that they are overcome with gratitude and thankfulness. And as You bless them, open their eyes to see and understand that every goodness in their life is from You. Work in _____'s life in such remarkable, real, and tangible ways that they can recognize these blessings could come only from You.

Do not let _____ believe that they are experiencing luck, karma, or good fortune based on anything else. Demolish any lies that would diminish Your gifts or _____'s understanding of the truth, so they can acknowledge You being at work in their life; and show gratitude and thanks to You.

Let these blessings show and confirm Your love for them personally.

Communicate that You haven't forgotten _____ or turned away from them, but that Your love is still strong and unconditional. Let this restatement of Your love and caring provision for them draw _____ back to revive their relationship with You. Amen.

## Chosen and Accepted

Isaiah 43:1, ***Do not fear, for I have redeemed you; I have called you by name, you are mine.***

Heavenly Father, help _____remember their true status in their relationship with You: that they are chosen and accepted. When _____ trusted You for their salvation, they became a new creation. Their identity is no longer what they do, but who they are: Your child, chosen and accepted.

They may have felt rejection by other people, or the world, which may have driven them into bad decisions and led them to places with people who were not good for them. But You have not, and You never will reject them. _____ has been adopted as sons/daughters of Yours, the Living God.

Help them know that this identity and value does not change with how far they have strayed from their path and relationship with You. But like the Prodigal Son, they need only turn to face their heavenly Father, and Your loving arms will be there, outstretched, welcoming them back into the fellowship of that heavenly relationship.

Lord, remind _____ of the truth that they do not need to clean up their act or have all their ducks in a row to return to You. Because You have chosen and accepted _____, You are there, waiting for them to simply call out to You. Help them call out to You. Amen.

## God's Faithfulness

Deuteronomy 7:9, *Know therefore that the Lord your God is God; he is the faithful God, keeping his covenant of love to a thousand generations of those who love him and keep his commandments.*

Heavenly Father, show _______ how You have been faithful in their life. Create a time where they can simply reflect on the past and recall times of Your involvement in their life when You were there and provided what they needed.

Thank You for the times You have been there for _______ in the past. When they did not see a way that anything good could come from their situation, reveal how You gave them Your perspective. Or at other times, provided:

wisdom

   understanding

      strength

         courage

            boldness

               perseverance

                  protection

                     encouragement

                        ...and answers to prayer.

Unveil places where You saved _______, delivered _______, or showed them a way to redeem or escape the situation when they could not think of a solution. Sometimes in the most unique way that no one else had even thought of.

Or maybe times when the circumstances didn't change, but even in the stress and hardship, You provided peace and calm that went beyond what others or the world could offer.

Let it build _______'s faith in Your ability and Your desire to help them in the future. Allow it to create a reassurance in Your godly ability to be with them wherever they go.

Knowing that You will never leave them and that Your love is everlasting and Your faithfulness is never ending; draw them back to You. Amen.

## *Reflections*

If you have been able to be consistent in praying this week — you are doing AMAZING!

If anything has gotten in your way, how can you remedy that?

_______________________________________________________________

In your prayer time this week, has God shown you anything about Himself? About the one you're praying for? About yourself?

_______________________________________________________________

_______________________________________________________________

_______________________________________________________________

Thinking back over the prayers you prayed this week…

Was there ever a time you felt God watching over you? Sensed His presence protecting you from something? Write it here and consider sharing it with someone — or the one you're praying for.

_______________________________________________________________

_______________________________________________________________

_______________________________________________________________

Psalm 35 is a great scripture for spiritual protection. See Appendix K (page 118) to personalize it for yourself or another person anytime you need it.

When have you faced a difficult circumstance? How did you respond and what did you learn?

_______________________________________________________________

_______________________________________________________________

_______________________________________________________________

Are there hurts from your past that you need to ask God to heal? Ask Him now.

_______________________________________________________________

_______________________________________________________________

_______________________________________________________________

How have you seen God at work in your life this week? If nothing comes to mind, spend a few minutes and ask Him to show you where He has protected or provided for you.

Consider starting a Faithfulness journal or making a Timeline of your life, indicating where God helped or directed you.


*Knowing* you are Chosen and Accepted is one thing, but *feeling* Chosen and Accepted is another. If you don't already *feel* it, ask God to help you with that.

I have heard: If God had a refrigerator, your picture would be on it! If He had a wallet, your photo would be in it! How does that make you feel? What makes you feel loved?

_______________________________________________________________________

_______________________________________________________________________

_______________________________________________________________________


If you have the opportunity to share with the one you're praying for, think about sharing something you learned from a difficult circumstance in your life, or how you recognized a negative influence and what you did to get away from it. Or *share how you see God at work in your life.*

Write about that here, or in the back of the book.

_______________________________________________________________________

_______________________________________________________________________

_______________________________________________________________________

_______________________________________________________________________

_______________________________________________________________________

_______________________________________________________________________

Have you sensed any pushback?

_______________________________________________

When you pray for another person, sometimes there is blowback on you and you may face hardship or discouragement yourself. It could be an upset with the one you're praying for – or any other relationship, or your work or home life. Maybe a sudden health issue or unexplained crisis. It may seem to come out of the blue, with no warning and no logic as to why things are happening. Praying for someone else does not make the evil one happy.

Have you experienced anything like that? What?

_______________________________________________

_______________________________________________

_______________________________________________

If this happens it's helpful to be sure you are praying on the Armor of God as part of your daily prayer time. Even a simple prayer like:

**Heavenly Father, thank You for the Armor You give me that protects me as I pray. I put on the Helmet of Salvation to protect my mind, and the Breastplate of Righteousness to protect my chest, organs, and heart. I put on the Belt of Truth to help me discern truth and reject any lies. I wear the Shoes of the Gospel of Peace and take up the Shield of Faith and the sword of the Spirit to fight in the battles You call me to. Amen.**

For more information see the Resource Guide on Spiritual Armor for Battle in Appendix B (page 102).

And pray for yourself, asking God to guard you and protect you, your family, your health, finances, relationships, home, job, and whatever else you feel led to pray about that could be attacked. Ask God to keep you standing firm.

It also helps to talk with another Christian friend and ask them to pray for you and what you're experiencing. And for the duration of this commitment.

## Find His Help Anywhere

Psalm 139:8-10,
*If I go up to the heavens, you are there;*
*if I make my bed in the depths, you are there.*
*If I rise on the wings of the dawn,*
*if I settle on the far side of the sea,*
*even there your hand will guide me,*
*your right hand will hold me fast.*

Heavenly Father, let _____ know that You are everywhere. Part of Your character is that You are omnipresent - which means "everywhere". There is no place on earth, in the depths of the earth or in the heavens where Your presence is not known or felt. In daylight and in darkness, You are there with _____.

Whether feeling alone, worried or afraid, remind _____ they can call on Your name at any moment of the day or night, from any place on earth - any country from the east to the west, any mountaintop or deepest cave or sea, You are there with them.

Thank You Lord that even if _____ is trying to hide from You, there is no limit to Your desire and ability to seek them out. You will go to great lengths to find, care for, love and help them. And in Your presence, all darkness is dispelled.

I praise You Lord, that _____ can never hide from Your love. Or wander from Your care. You are God Almighty and You are everywhere. _____ is never alone. Help _____ understand that even if they are tempted, or even if they fall, even if they follow Your direction halfway or run the other way, that You will meet them where they are. That You will love them like before. Because they can never hide from Your love. Amen.

**Keep from Stumbling**

Jude 1:24, *To him who is able to keep you from stumbling and to present you before his glorious presence without fault and with great joy...*

Heavenly Father, reveal the path to ______ for a return to You and to living a godly life again. Remove any stumbling blocks that would keep ______ away or deter them from the narrow path that leads back to You.

If there are influences in ______'s life that would prevent them seeing You or calling out to You, remove those. If there are any plans of the evil one that would seek to keep ______ in dark captivity or idolatry, demolish those!

When ______ calls out to You, answer them quickly with an easily discernable voice they recognize and completely understand. And let that communication be so unique and spectacular that ______ has no doubt it came from You - their Creator and Savior!

Father, in turning from the values of the world and evil influences, there will be temptations where people or the world, the evil one or even ______'s own flesh will want to draw them back in to the old way of living. Strengthen ______'s commitment and their faith, and determination to follow You.

Reward even the smallest steps they take in Your direction. Take them over, under, around, or through obstacles, temptations, and deliver them from any traps set for them. As You draw them to You, give ______ sure footing on the path, and light their way back to You. Amen.

## Use Circumstances

Genesis 50:20, *Joseph said...“You intended to harm me, but God intended it for good.”*

Heavenly Father, please use the circumstances in _____'s life to draw them to You. Call their attention to the big broad strokes You've painted their life with and the tiny brush strokes that make up the details. It could be the big events or even the smaller, everyday routine occurrences that create and feed their desire to refocus and turn back to You.

Where there is joy in _____'s life, let them see that it's not just good luck or their own efforts that have brought the joy. Let them see beyond the circumstance or seeming coincidence, to the power behind the blessing that comes from You.

And if there are difficult conditions, or even tragic sorrows, do not let those be wasted. Regardless of what brought them on: their own bad decisions, the work or influence of the evil one, or mere happenstance; use those to get ____'s attention. Like the Prodigal son in the pig sty in Luke 15:11-32, let _____'s circumstances confront them in a way that can't be ignored.

Don't let any turmoil they have gone through keep them on a dark path. Don't let it be lost or unproductive. But use it to bring _____ back into a close relationship with You.

Father, I would love to see _____ drawn to You by blessing and joy. But I understand that even with me, sometimes You have to use other measures to get my attention. Please do whatever it takes to bring _____ to You, to hear and accept Your invitation and direction back to faith. Amen.

### Receive Forgiveness

Psalm 103:10-11,
>*he does not treat us as our sins deserve*
>>*or repay us according to our iniquities.*
>*For as high as the heavens are above the earth,*
>>*so great is his love for those who fear him;*
>*as far as the east is from the west,*
>>*so far has he removed our transgressions from us.*

Romans 3:23-24, *for all have sinned and fall short of the glory of God, and all are justified freely by his grace through the redemption that came by Christ Jesus.*

**H**eavenly Father, remind _______ that when they *confess their sin, You are faithful and just and will forgive them of their sin, and cleanse them from any unrighteousness* (1 John 1:9). And let that draw them back to You.

Thank You, that You do not overwhelm _______ with a realization of all their sin at once, but gently lead them to a knowledge and understanding of it. In Your timing, bring to mind those sins of thought, attitude, speech, relationships, rebellion, acts they have committed, or things they failed to do that they should have. And break _______'s heart over their sin. Turn them away from the thoughts and attitudes that brought them to those places and led them to those actions.

Bring _______ in humility to Your feet to name their sin, turn away from it, and ask for, and receive Your forgiveness.

Father, once forgiven by You _______ may still have a hard time forgiving themself. Help them let go of any anger, sadness, guilt, or shame they may still feel. If they still hear a harsh voice inside their head, remind _______ they are only human and will make mistakes again. Show them how to give themselves permission to be fallible.

Show them how to treat themself with kindness and the same forgiveness You have already given them. And help _______ walk in that freedom of forgiveness.

Remind _______ that they are loved, chosen, accepted, forgiven, and free from condemnation. And that You are with them always, to help them make wise choices and encourage them on their path. Amen.

## Offer Forgiveness

Matthew 6:14-15, *For if you forgive other people when they sin against you, your heavenly Father will also forgive you. But if you do not forgive others their sins, your Father will not forgive your sins.*

Heavenly Father, if _______ is harboring unforgiveness in their heart towards anyone who has caused them pain; physical, psychological, mental, financial, or emotional - by accident, through misunderstanding, by intention or malice, lead them to forgive the offender.

_______ may feel like if they forgive someone who's hurt them or their family, they're letting the offender get away with something, releasing them from the consequences or punishment of their hurtful actions. This can make forgiving someone very hard.

Holding on to hurts can make _______ bitter, hard-hearted, sad, and depressed. The analogy is true that it's like they are drinking poison and expecting the other person to die! _______ is the one who is most affected by their own unforgiveness.

Romans 12:19 says: *Do not take revenge, my dear friends, but leave room for God's wrath, for it is written: 'It is mine to avenge; I will repay,' says the Lord.*

Father, bring someone into _______'s life who can show them how to forgive. Who can lead them to You, or to the Bible, to see the freedom they will have with forgiveness. And help them say those words, "I forgive them," that will free them from the prison of unforgiveness.

It may not be wise for _______ to confront the person who hurt them. Lord, show them how to handle what needs to happen for forgiveness to occur. Maybe only a conversation with You, or a friend or counselor is necessary.

Help them bring every offense they've suffered to You, Lord, and follow Your lead.

Heavenly Father there are times when we even harbor anger and unforgiveness against You. If there is anything _______ believes You may have done or failed to do in their life, help them fully express that to You as well. Heal their emotions, show them how to let go of any resentment. And let them walk in the victory of forgiveness. Amen.

## See God in His Creation

Romans 1:20, *For since the creation of the world God's invisible qualities — his eternal power and divine nature — have been clearly seen, being understood from what has been made...*

Heavenly Father, lead _______ to see You in their everyday environment — Your Creation! There are so many ways You are with us — directing and protecting, guiding and guarding, encouraging and uplifting us that we miss. Let _______ recognize and acknowledge how You are with them every day.

Your power and divine characteristics are made known and reflected in Your Creation. And many people feel closer to You when they take time to notice animals, plants, weather, mountains, lakes, oceans.

Let _______ see You in nature on a hike in the mountains, a walk in the woods, sitting by the beach, watching an animal or storm, listening quietly to the natural sounds around them or gazing out a window at clouds in a sunrise or sunset. And give recognition and glory not to what was made, but to You, the Maker.

Let _______ be amazed by the environment around them and gain a sense that there is something much bigger, more powerful, creative, and good at work in the world and in their life that they can connect to.

Teach _______ that You speak through Your Creation. By paying attention to what they see, hear, smell, or can touch, lead them to ask what You might be saying to them about Yourself, about their life, or a message You want them to hear. An ant, a flower, a storm, can all be a lesson, a model, a warning, a revelation.

Father, richly reward their attention to Your messages through Your Creation. Help _______ see and understand. Amen.

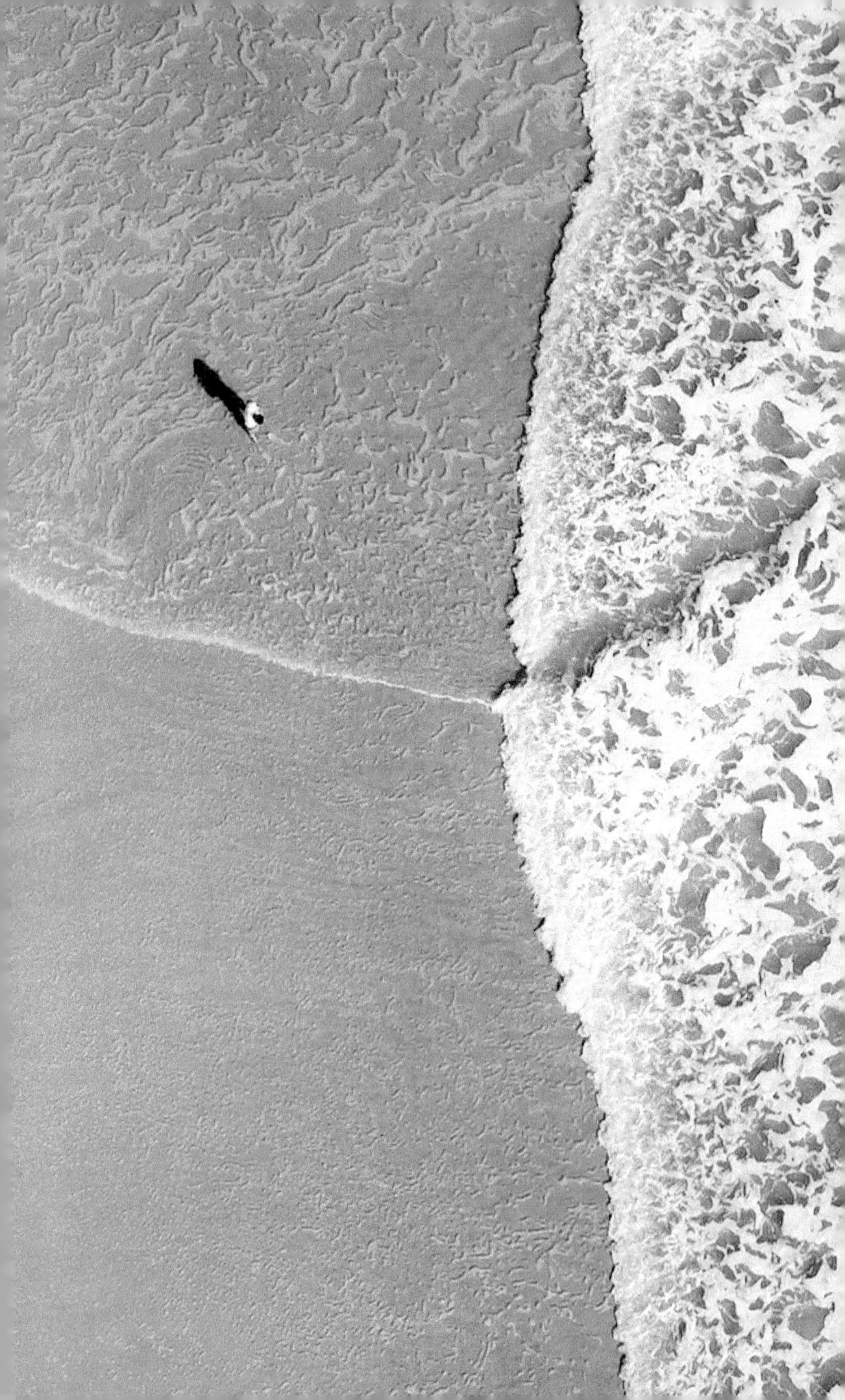

## Spiritual Reconnection

John 15:5, *I am the vine; you are the branches. If you remain in me and I in you, you will bear much fruit; apart from me you can do nothing.*

**H**eavenly Father, let ______ be a branch that is connected to You, the Vine. Draw them close to You, connecting with You to draw life from You.

John 15 explains how the branches need to stay connected to the vine to have life and vitality. ______ has drifted away from You and is no longer bearing fruit. Help ______ move closer to You again, and remain in You to be fruitful.

Do not let ______ continue to reject You when You give direction in their life. Help them hear Your voice of leading and encouragement and accept that over what the world tells them. And not become a branch that is cut off, withers and is thrown into the fire. Help them see that what they can accomplish apart from You is nothing compared to the fruit they can bear with You.

Renew in ______ a desire to read Your Word, spend time in prayer, get involved with other believers, and get out to experience Your Creation.

Father, get ______'s attention now. Open their ears to hear Your voice, and call them back to fellowship with You, to remain in You, to abide in You.

Abiding is a continuous, ongoing action. In the good times and in the hard times of stress and trial, ______ will get what they need if they abide, stay connected to You, the Vine. Help ______ reconnect. Amen.

# *Reflections*

You are doing AMAZING!  Way to go for 28 days!
If anything has gotten in your way, remedy that and keep going!

In your prayer time this week, has God shown you anything about Himself? About the one you're praying for? About yourself?

_______________________________________________

_______________________________________________

Thinking back over the prayers you prayed this week...
Whatever path you're on, there will be stumbling blocks and circumstances to overcome. Even if you're off the path, God can find and help you anywhere. How has God gotten you "over, under, around, or through" an obstacle? Or how has He used something negative in your life to turn it into something positive?

_______________________________________________

_______________________________________________

_______________________________________________

If _______ is going through a hard time, encourage them that God is in control and can work even what was meant for harm, for good. Maybe send a card or text to cheer them.

God coaches us to win! He will seek us out and forgive our sin and restore us. Is there anything you need forgiveness for? Write that down — be specific and detailed if necessary — and ask for God's forgiveness now.

_______________________________________________

_______________________________________________

_______________________________________________

Have you experienced the bitterness of unforgiveness? Have you received the freedom that comes from forgiving?
Ask God to show you if there is anyone you need to forgive and jot down their initials.

_______________________________________________

Ask God for His help in forgiving that person. Check out the Appendix J (page 116) on Forgiveness to better understand how and why forgiveness sets YOU free.

Make a list of situations or persons and bring them before the Lord in prayer. Ask God how He would lead you in your circumstances.

Share a way God's Creation has spoken to you.

What are some ways you reconnect with God when it's been a while?

## Be their Refuge

Psalm 91:1-2, ***Whoever dwells in the shelter of the Most High will rest in the shadow of the Almighty. I will say of the Lord, "He is my refuge and my fortress, my God, in whom I trust."***

Heavenly Father, as _______ begins to see You in their everyday life, be the refuge they go to when they feel overwhelmed. Offer them the security, protection, shelter, help, and provision they need from any danger, trouble, threat or attack that comes from the evil one, the world, or even from their own thoughts or feelings.

The flesh, the world, and the evil one are all influences that war against Your wisdom, Your plan and Your purpose for _______'s life. The evil one seeks to keep them fearful, frustrated, discouraged, and overwhelmed, and make their faith in You waver because of difficult circumstances.

These forces desire _______'s financial ruin, the destruction of relationships, the smearing of their reputation, and personal moral failure. The enemy is always crouching at their door, waiting to devour them.

But You Heavenly Father, will come to their aid. You are more powerful than any other force in the universe! You can protect and deliver _______ from attacks of the evil one, from the ungodly influences of the world, and the temptations and discouragements of their flesh.

Call _______ to a place of peace, a time of rest, a safe and calm respite amidst whatever storm they're facing. Remind them to call on Your name and enter into a sacred space and time of communicating with You through Your Bible, prayer, worship, and receive Your peace.

Reassure _______ they can call on You and trust in You to be their refuge. Amen.

### Help them Run the Race

Hebrews 12:1-2, *Therefore...let us throw off everything that hinders and the sin that so easily entangles. And let us run with perseverance the race marked out for us, fixing our eyes on Jesus, the pioneer and perfecter of our faith.*

**H**eavenly Father, point out anything in _____'s life that is a hindrance to their being obedient to You, so they can follow the course You have laid out for them.

I know You give _____ choices. And there are many ways and things they could do to spend the time and energy You have given them. But I believe that when _____ is able to use the talents and spiritual gifts You have placed in them specifically, they will experience more growth and more fruitfulness.

Lead them back to the path You have laid out for them. Help _____ fix their eyes on You, look to You for direction. Open their eyes to see You, and all You have to show them.

Lord, in Psalm 112 You say that _____ will be blessed when they fear You, and find great delight in Your commands. So let _____ remember to respect and honor You. Let them be generous and conduct their affairs with justice so good will come to them.

On the path You have for _____, even in darkness, light will dawn for them when they are gracious, compassionate, and righteous. And _____ will not be shaken as You rebuild their faith. Draw them to You, Lord. Teach them. Let them know Your voice and feel Your love.

Father, give _____ the perseverance they need to refocus on You, and bring them again, onto the path You have for them. Bring people and circumstances into their life that will make them stronger, better, more obedient followers. Use others as iron to sharpen them to be useful tools in Your mighty hands. Amen.

## Opportunities for Godly Fellowship

Matthew 18:20, *For where two or three gather in my name, there am I with them.*

Heavenly Father, help _____ find fellowship with other believers, and find a place to use the gifts and talents You have given them in godly ways for good. Give _____ opportunities to see and hear others sharing their belief in You, talking about their faith experiences, and the ways You are impacting their life for good, and getting them through hard times.

It may have been a while since they attended a church service, and may feel awkward at first, but encourage _____ to accept an invitation to go to a church, a worship service, a small group Bible study session, a holiday event or presentation. Open a door to a Bible believing fellowship where they can learn and have their faith rekindled.

Show _____ where there are other believers in places they already go or people they work with or know. Encourage those relationships and strengthen the bonds between _____ and other godly people.

Father, I ask that You lead _____ to a fellowship and a Bible teaching congregation where they can use the spiritual blessings and gifts You've given them. And when they go to those places or churches, or meet with believers, give _____ joy and a revival of their faith. Amen.

## Courage

Joshua 1:9, *Have I not commanded you? Be strong and courageous. Do not be afraid; do not be discouraged, for the Lord your God will be with you wherever you go.*

Heavenly Father, give _____ courage, strength to overcome any discouragement, depression, anxiety they have in order to embrace the new path You have for them.

Quiet the voices of the world and the enemy who want to keep _____ fearful, discouraged and overwhelmed. Do not let fear get the better of them but help _____ seek out Your promises and hold to those even in the face of trials and trouble.

Do not let _____ compare the size of any enemy or situation to their own strength and be filled with fear and dread. Remind them to compare every enemy to the size and strength of their great God who has promised them an abundant life — You!

When _____ looks at their circumstances, remind them they are not alone that they can call on You — their Ally:

- The One who can do miracles!

- The One who keeps His promises!

- The One who is faithful to His Word!

Help _____ realize that when You are with them, they are totally protected from the enemy. Lead _____ into their promised land and help them take possession of it. Do not let them delay, but go quickly in obedience and courage to follow You. Father, strengthen _____ with Your courage. Amen

## Strength

**Ephesians 3:16, *I pray that out of his glorious riches he may strengthen you with power through his Spirit in your inner being.***

Heavenly Father, You own the cattle on a thousand hills! The earth and everything in it, is Yours. And not just Your right of Sovereignty over the wealth of all things, but the richness of Your character also allows You the ability to pour over _____ all that they might ever need.

So Father, as _____ turns to You in big and small ways, strengthen them:

***Physically:*** Give them Your healing in all the areas of their body where there is illness or weakness. Increase their strength and stamina to be able to do the work You set before them.

***Mentally:*** When _____ needs to focus, or clear their mind of distracting thoughts. Give them the ability and the diligence to take every thought captive to You, and to be alert to dangers around them. Do not let _____'s thinking become muddled by the vain philosophies of man or the half-truths and lies of the evil one.

***Emotionally:*** Give _____ relief from discouragement, sadness, fear, anger, guilt, anxiety and depression. Help them deal with their circumstances according to Your wisdom and not be led by their emotions.

***Spiritually:*** Bolster _____'s faith with the remembrance that no matter what — You are on their side! That no matter what things look like from an earthly perspective, You are in control! And give them spiritual strength to recognize and combat the enemy, dressed in their spiritual armor.

Thank You that You are able to do immeasurably more that I can ask or even imagine, according to Your power that is at work in _____. I give You all the glory and praise, for ever and ever. (Ephesians 3:21) Amen.

## Divine Appointments

Philippians 2:13, ***For it is God who works in you to will and to act in order to fulfill his good purpose.***

Heavenly Father, You created the universe! Create "Divine Appointments" in _____ 's life. Arrange opportunities for them to be in the right place at the right time to hear or see something or someone who will contribute to understanding Your love for _____ and Your provision and purpose for their life.

Let _____ witness events or casual occurrences that make a connection with You and Your power, or truths they learned from the Bible. Do not let Your Word return void! Create a constant stream of positive, godly and encouraging direction for _____.

Whether they discover something helpful in a podcast, or the theme of a movie, a real-life discussion, or an unexpected circumstance, bring them experiences that apply biblical faith and truth to their work life, their relationships, their home and social and spiritual life.

Orchestrate meetings with others who can introduce them to the answers they're looking for. Lead _____ to people who can enlighten, teach, direct, encourage, support, and be a resource and blessing to them. And help them deepen the connection that You are providing for them.

Let these Divine Appointments benefit them to the point of sensing Your presence in blessing their life. And when these Appointments occur, don't let _____ miss the significance of what is happening. But open their mind, heart and spirit to the influences You bring their way. Amen.

FOLLOW

**Mentors and Role Models**

1 Corinthians 11:1, *Follow my example as I follow the example of Christ.*

Heavenly Father, bring spiritual mentors and role models into _____'s life. Let their mentors be someone who is spiritually mature and can counsel and support them from a position of godly wisdom and experience. You know the kind of person that can impact and influence _____ best. Send someone they will respect and listen to who will make an impression on them even where they are right now.

Provide opportunities for mentors to take an active interest in _____'s life; and to observe and speak into all kinds of issues and situations they face. Give these mentors Your wisdom to know how to interact with and be involved with _____ in a natural, relaxed way.

Father, provide godly role models who will speak the truth and show _____ how to live a godly life in this ungodly world. Let these people demonstrate how to make wise decisions. Let their behavior speak into _____'s life of how to live out godly values, even if others around them are not.

Let _____ observe their mentor attending a Bible teaching church, reading the Bible, praying, sharing fellowship with other believers. Perhaps even get involved in community outreach to people in need, or going on a mission trip to another country.

Show, and let _____ see and imitate people who live with integrity, honesty, kindness, courage, faith, and self-control. Lead _____ to recognize and embrace those who You've placed in their life to help guide and encourage them.

Father, thank You for the way You use ordinary people in our lives for extraordinary purposes. Let _____ 's faith grow and be strengthened by every encounter with believers, role models, and mentors. Amen.

# *Reflections*

You are almost there!! Great job! — You are AWESOME!

In your prayer time this week, has God shown you anything about Himself? About the one you're praying for? About yourself?

_______________________________________________

_______________________________________________

_______________________________________________

_______________________________________________

Thinking back over the prayers you prayed this week...

When have you had to rely on God for Strength? Courage? A Refuge? Or help staying on the path, "running the race" He has for you?

_______________________________________________

_______________________________________________

_______________________________________________

_______________________________________________

Have you had Divine Appointments? Something that just happened to work out where you felt God must've orchestrated it?

_______________________________________________

_______________________________________________

_______________________________________________

_______________________________________________

Share your answers to one of these questions with someone this week.

Do you have a role model or mentor in your life? Or are you a role model or mentor for someone else? Who?

_______________________________________________

_______________________________________________

_______________________________________________

_______________________________________________

If so, how do you make time to spend with them?

_______________________________________________________

_______________________________________________________

_______________________________________________________

_______________________________________________________

Let them know how your 40 Day Journey has been going.

If you don't have a role model or mentor, ask God to bring someone who can share your desire to pray and be accountable in your commitments.

And if you are not a role model or mentor for someone else, ask God to bring someone you can pour your life into.

**Psalm 20**

**Psalm 20:1, *May the Lord answer you when you are in distress.***

**O** *Lord, answer _____ when they are in distress.* Place in their heart the desire to call out to You, and let them hear Your voice above all else going on in their life. Thank You that You are never too busy to hear _____'s cry for help. And thank You that You can handle any kind of distress possible.

Whether _____ is physically ill, hurt, weak or weary, You can help. If they are in an emotional state of anxiety, sadness, depression, worry, fear, or grief, You can handle it. If there is spiritual turmoil or confusion, or they are feeling tempted, lift them up.

*May the name of the God of Jacob protect _____.* Father, protect _____'s life, their health, their relationships, their mind, their emotions, their spirit, their work, their comings and their goings. There is great power in Your name. Yahweh! Jehovah! Jesus! Almighty God! El Shaddai! Adonai!

*May You send _____ help from the sanctuary* where You sit enthroned and have angels as Your messengers to do Your bidding, *"and grant them support from Zion."* Wherever _____ is, You can reach them with just the help they need. Your help is better than any the world can offer. You can deliver them from anything and help them bear up under any circumstance or oppression.

*May You remember all _____'s sacrifices and accept their burnt offerings.* The sacrifices You desire are obedience and a contrite, repentant heart. A burnt offering is one that is offered up totally, completely consumed in the fire. May _____'s life be entirely and wholly offered to You. Lead them to a place where their words, actions, and attitudes all honor You.

*Would You give _____ the desires of their heart* and remove any desires that would take them away from or would not honor You. *And make all their plans succeed* as You direct their steps.

*Some trust in chariots and some in horses, but lead _____ to trust in the name of the Lord their God.* What is considered power and might in the world are worthless compared to Your power and might. Do not let _____ place their trust in world leaders, politicians, athletes, business moguls or any other person of influence. Or find their sense of security in money, fame, position, good looks, or good health. But trust in You alone. Because You alone are trustworthy.

*I will shout for joy when You bring victory to _____'s life, and will lift up our banners in the name of our God!* Amen!

FIRM GRIP

## Establish the Work of Their Hands

Psalm 90:17, *May the favor of the Lord our God rest on us; establish the work of our hands for us.*

Heavenly Father, You have created and gifted ______ with specific talents, abilities, passions and experiences that make them one of a kind. They have unique gifts and strengths from You they are not using. It's such a waste when they could find great purpose and success in using those talents You have created them for.

Lord show ______ some work, vocational or otherwise, that uses, encourages, and celebrates the specific way You created them. And lead them to opportunities to be involved with projects or ministries, organizations or businesses that need their talents and benefit from them.

Working in areas that don't use what You've given ______ as strengths, let them find it draining, frustrating and unsatisfying work. Draw them to opportunities their gifts and talents connect with and let them see Your hand in it.

Let ______ see that the more they use their gifts, the more they will be developed. And they will have the experience of feeling fulfilled, working at something they're good at.

Help ______ make that joyful connection: that when they use those gifts and talents You blessed them with, they experience satisfaction and success.

Let that draw them even closer to You, Lord, wanting to know You more, and how You made them. And let that lead them to find a meaningful purpose for their life, in You. Amen.

## Take Hold of Gifts and Affirmation

James 1:17, *Every good and perfect gift is from above, coming down from the Father...*

1 Peter 4:10, *Each of you should use whatever gift you have received to serve others...*

Heavenly Father, You have given _____ so many gifts and blessings: from Your Son offering eternal life, to physical things like our bodies and minds, to character gifts like courage, resilience, or caring, to spiritual gifts like discernment, wisdom, and the Fruit of the Spirit. But we need to accept them - take hold of them, to receive them from You in order to use them.

Father, loosen _____'s grasp on whatever else they're holding on to so tightly so their hands are open to receive what You have for them. In all aspects of their life, let them see and appreciate all You have given them. Whatever they're holding on to that they think is of value, cannot compare to the greater gifts You want to give them.

As _____ accepts and uses these gifts, it will help them face and overcome the world. They can be Overcomers through You because You have overcome the world.

Father, I ask for another gift for _____. As they turn back to You, please give them an affirmation they are on the right path. Let it be a real and tangible indication they will recognize as coming from You. Something that will act as a sign post along their path that shows they're headed in the right direction.

Let it be an encouragement that they can still discern Your voice and Your leading in their life. Lord, You know _____ better than I do, so whatever affirmation or gift You choose, I know it will be perfect for them. Amen.

## Lay Them on the Altar

Genesis 22:2, ***Then God said, "Take your son, your only son, whom you love — Isaac — and go to the region of Moriah. Sacrifice him there as a burnt offering on a mountain I will show you."***

Heavenly Father, I admit that no matter how deeply I love _____ and want them to experience a return to You and a joyful spirit-filled life, I cannot make it happen. Only You can do all that.

I'm so grateful that You already know the good plans You have for _____'s life — to prosper them and not harm them, but to give _____ hope and a future (Jeremiah 29:11).

Just as You commanded Abraham to lay Isaac on the sacrificial altar, I acknowledge that _____ is Your child. They mean the world to me, so I lay _____ on the altar as a sacrifice to say that I acknowledge Your control of their life; and all the factors that affect their attitudes and decision-making processes. I surrender my hopes and dreams for them, and whatever influence or sway I may have imagined I have with them and I leave them in Your capable and loving hands.

I know You will protect Your precious child _____ from evil. Thank You in advance for directing their path to use the gifts and talents You have given them to allow them to fulfill the purpose You created them for. As the stars shine bright in the sky, shine brightly in _____'s life and heart and spirit to dispel any darkness around them — whatever the source.

I give You thanks and praise in advance, and wait, anticipating the miracles You will work in _____'s life. Amen.

## Aaronic Blessing

Numbers 6:24–26, *The Lord bless you and keep you...*

Heavenly Father, as Aaron, the High Priest, gave this blessing over the people of Israel, I pray it now over _____ as I finish this amazing prayer journey. I pray this blessing as a reassuring reminder, not only of Your amazing and powerful presence and protection for them, but of Your desire and ability to fulfill the purpose You created them for.

Defining the six Hebrew verbs adds a deeper understanding of the blessing's meaning. These expanded definitions of this blessing's Hebrew verbs come from Bill Bullock, The Rabbi's Son. Find him on www.biblicallifestylecenter.org

- *Bless:* May You, Lord God, the Holy One, infuse _____ with unlimited potential and power and release them from any restrictions or limitations that would prevent them from reaching the fullness of their potential to participate in their divine purpose which You have given them.

- *Keep:* May You zealously cherish and treasure _____ diligently defending and keeping watch over them to protect and save them.

- *Shine His Face:* May the light of Your innermost being and essence illuminate _____ physiologically and spiritually, impacting their body, mind, soul and spirit with Your warming, healing, soothing, restorative, empowering and constantly renewing energy.

- *Graciousness:* May You, the Holy One, give _____ what they really need, not out of pity, benevolence, generosity or some misguided thought that they have earned it, but because You have promised, as the stronger covenant partner, to strengthen them and enable them to reach their potential and enjoy the covenant You entered into with them, when they accepted You as Savior.

- *His Countenance:* As You were in the Holy of Holies, may You be present with _____ so they can experience true spiritual reality.

- *Peace:* And may You place in and establish in _____ wholeness, wellness, purposeful living in joy, with abundant provision, harmony, safety, security summed up in the Hebrew word "shalom."

## The "Priestly Blessing"

### *Y'varechecha Adonai*

[May the Holy One bless you]

### *v'yish'merecha*

[and zealously cherish and keep watch over you]

### *Ya'er Adonai panav elecha*

[May the Holy One's Face shine upon you]

### *v'chuneka*

[and shower you with grace]

### *Yisa Adonai panav elecha*

[May the Holy One lift up His countenance upon you]

### *v'yasem lecha shalom*

[and may He give you wholeness, wellness,
security, abundant provision, and peace]

## (Numbers 6:24-26)

# *Reflections*

**CONGRATULATIONS! YOU MADE IT!**
You've finished the Journey you started!  You did it!  The whole 40 Days!!
We are so very proud of you!
How does it feel?

_______________________________________________

Thinking back over the prayers you prayed this week...

Have you placed someone's name in scripture before? I believe God loves when we pray His words back to Him. Simply replace the pronouns with those of the person you're praying for, or their name. Refer to Appendix K (page 118) for another example of how to personalize Scripture.

How are you using you gifts and talents?

_______________________________________________

_______________________________________________

If you're not, take hold of those gifts and ask God to show you a way, a place, and an opportunity to do that.

How have you discerned God's voice of affirmation? Or the opposite, when He's redirecting you?

_______________________________________________

_______________________________________________

Laying someone on the altar is challenging. Ask God to help you remember you are the tool in the Master's hand. He is the Master.

During your 40 Day Prayer Journey, has God shown you anything new about Himself?

_______________________________________________

_______________________________________________

How will you apply that to your life?

_______________________________________________

_______________________________________________

Have you learned anything new about the one you prayed for?

_______________________________________________

_______________________________________________

Will that change the way you think about or interact with them?

_______________________________________________

_______________________________________________

Has God shown you anything new about yourself?

_______________________________________________

_______________________________________________

Do you feel any differently about prayer?

_______________________________________________

_______________________________________________

About the way God works in others?

_______________________________________________

_______________________________________________

In you?

_______________________________________________

_______________________________________________

Have a time of Thanksgiving! Think about these past 40 Days or the past year. Give God thanks in prayer for ways you've seen Him at work in your life or the one you prayed for; blessings or protections, answers to prayer:

Is there another person God has led you to pray these 40 Days again for?
Or is there another 40 Day Prayer Guide that will bless someone else? Or even yourself?

**_Praying for Someone's Salvation_**

**_Praying a Blessing for Someone_**

**_Praying for Godly Character_**

**_Praying for Your Grandchild_**

**_Praying for Your Pastor_**

**_Praying to Recover from a Mistake_**

Lastly, have you come to this point, thinking that nothing seems different? Nothing seems to have changed? We hear you. Flip to Post-Journey Check-in (page 98) for some encouraging thoughts on why this is not the end of the story.

## Thank You After 40 Days

**H**eavenly Father, thank You for this journey of praying intentionally and consistently for _______ these 40 days. It is wonderful to have covered them in prayer so intentionally and consistently. Thank You for Your help in keeping me faithful on this journey. And for the things you have shown me while spending time with You.

Thank You for Your promise to hear me when I call to You. And to answer my prayers.

I believe Your Word will not return void, but will go out and continue to be at work in _______'s life. I pray Your power will be released to accomplish the work of helping _______ make their way back to You and rekindle their faith and godly way of living. Show them in large and small, tangible ways, how they're moving in the right direction.

Father, continue to reveal Your truth to them. Don't let them forget what You've shown them and what they've learned in these 40 days.

Thank You for hearing and answering my prayers - in ways that are above and beyond what I could ever ask for or even imagine. Show me if there is someone else I need to be praying for — even for myself. And be with me on that journey as well. Amen.

# Post-Journey Check-in

*What if I'm at the end of praying for this person and have seen nothing? No change at all.*

We hear you, and don't worry. You've given this all over to God, including His timeframe for resolving it. That said, *you have to know* the last 40 days have had an impact. Doors are opening. Wheels are in motion. Let's look at two very real possibilities –

1. There are deeper issues that may require working through some complex matters with a professional. Sports athletes realize their top performance working with sports coaches. Same with us. Part of the solution may be with a Counselor.

2. There *has* been change, and God is working something amazing in their life, but it's going to take longer than 40 days to bring it to completion. What's your part in this continuing process? Watering the seeds from this journey.

Remember Jesus' parable about the seeds?

*When anyone hears the message about the kingdom and does not understand it, the evil one comes and snatches away what was sown in their heart. This is the seed sown along the path. The seed falling on rocky ground refers to someone who hears the word and at once receives it with joy. But since they have no root, they last only a short time. When trouble or persecution comes because of the word, they quickly fall away. The seed falling among the thorns refers to someone who hears the word, but the worries of this life and the deceitfulness of wealth choke the word, making it unfruitful. But the seed falling on good soil refers to someone who hears the word and understands it. This is the one who produces a crop, yielding a hundred, sixty or thirty times what was sown.*
Matt 13:19-23

So we're talking about restoration and healing here, and not necessarily salvation, but I think the same principles apply. What does the heart and soul of your person look like right now? Are they a hardened prodigal, doubling down on their decision to sleep with the pigs, rather than admit they're wrong and return home?

Trust that seeds have been planted in this time. No question. And whether it's many, or just a few, all they need is watering and they will grow:

- Grow into dissatisfaction with their current circumstances.

- Grow into desires for more than they have been living for.

- Grow into a calling to a life with far more meaning and purpose.

- Grow into a desire to restore their relationship with Jesus and others.

You and I simply cannot fathom God's plans for your Wanderer on this side of eternity, but the fact remains, you have prayed and petitioned Almighty God to take action in this person's life, so we can trust that this is happening.

What you've started is a powerful force for change in their world. Pray that these seeds are watered – by circumstance, chance meetings, and people in their life. That they begin to take root and grow, changing their thinking and perspectives. Spawning new ideas and dreams for their life. Stay with it.

You can even pull out the big guns, going back to Day 2 and praying this book through for them again. And again. Maybe consider the *40 Days: Salvation* book listed in the ending Reflections instead?

Sin and shame has no chance against the prayers of a righteous person. Be patient. Be faithful. Wait for it.

*But while he was still a long way off, his father saw him and was filled with compassion for him; he ran to his son, threw his arms around him and kissed him.* Luke 15:20

God has plans for this person. You are playing a part in all of it. Good job. Now watch carefully and see what results — in God's timing, and to the praise of our Glorious Lord.

# *Appendix A: Confession and Repentance*

Let God speak to you now and show you any sin you need to confess. Psalm 66:18 tells us if we cherish sin in our hearts, God won't listen to our prayers. Tell God you are willing to turn away from those things (which is repentance) and ask for His forgiveness.

But 1 John 1:9-10 tells us "If we confess our sins, He is faithful and righteous to forgive us our sins and to cleanse us from all unrighteousness. If we claim we have not sinned, we make Him a liar, and His word is not in us."

Ask God if there are sins of:

THOUGHT — impure, selfish, angry, fearful, jealous

ATTITUDE — prideful, judgmental, argumentative, lukewarm toward God

SPEECH — crude, inappropriate, grumbling, divisive, lies, half-truths

RELATIONSHIP — wrong or improper, physically or emotionally
> Do you need to forgive someone? Do you need to ask for forgiveness?
> As a husband: are you providing spiritual leadership, guiding and nurturing your wife?
> As a wife: are you honoring and respecting your husband?
> As parents: are you modeling godly behavior and attitudes and teaching your children in love?
> As children or teens: are you respectful and obedient?

COMMISSION — things that you have done, actions you have taken
> Have you done something you know is wrong?
> Do you guard your eyes?
> Have you exposed yourself to the occult?
> Do you have habits that are harmful to your body/mind/spirit?

OMISSION – things you have failed to do
> Has God prompted you to do something you haven't?
> Have you failed to do good when you could have?

SELF-RULE – rebellion, going your own way
> Are you following God or going your own way?
> Are you avoiding something He's told you to do?
> Or are you still doing something He's told you not to?

# Appendix B: Spiritual Armor for Battle

Ephesians 6:10-18, *Finally, be strong in the Lord and in his mighty power. Put on the full armor of God, so that you can take your stand against the devil's schemes. For our struggle is not against flesh and blood, but against the rulers, against the authorities, against the powers of this dark world and against the spiritual forces of evil in the heavenly realms. Therefore put on the full armor of God, so that when the day of evil comes, you may be able to stand your ground, and after you have done everything, to stand. Stand firm then, with the belt of truth buckled around your waist, with the breastplate of righteousness in place, and with your feet fitted with the readiness that comes from the gospel of peace. In addition to all this, take up the shield of faith, with which you can extinguish all the flaming arrows of the evil one. Take the helmet of salvation and the sword of the Spirit, which is the word of God.*

*And pray in the Spirit on all occasions with all kinds of prayers and requests. With this in mind, be alert and always keep on praying for all the Lord's people.*

We dress ourselves in the armor Paul describes here. He wrote his letter to the Ephesians while he was in Rome under house arrest, guarded by Roman soldiers. Every day, he saw men dressed in armor, bearing the insignia of their authority. The Holy Spirit must have inspired his analogy of a Christian "soldier."

***Praying on the armor can be as simple as
listing each piece and stating that you are putting it on and wearing it.***

When we are praying for someone, or even ourselves, the devil doesn't like it. And even with his limited power here on earth, we can find ourselves under attack in ways that can lead us to feel discouraged, defeated, even want to give up.

But we rely on the fact that God's armor is the very best!

The **Belt of Truth** is a wide, tight band around the waist that holds pieces of the armor on as well as the sword. It provides support for the back and core. When we are "girded" with truth we can more easily recognize the lies the devil would tempt us to believe. We will not be mesmerized by half-truths or deceptions.

The **Breastplate of Righteousness** protects our heart and vital organs, a kind of forerunner of the bulletproof vest. It stops and deflects stabs and projectiles, keeping our heart and spirit from evil deceptions. Our righteousness comes from Jesus Christ. His blood paid the price for our sin and we gain the righteousness of the perfect life He lived. In that righteousness the devil cannot hold anything against us.

The **Shoes of the Gospel of Peace** help us walk in the Spirit. Putting on shoes is a sign of readiness and preparedness. With these we are ready to carry the Good News of salvation and peace into our relationships and whatever challenges we face. With our feet protected like this we will have traction even when we feel unsteady, and will be able to stand firm.

The **Shield of Faith** is not some puny little garbage can lid with a handle; but a head-to-toe protection, repelling the enemy's offensive weapons. When the shield was anointed with oil it would reflect the glare of the sun and blind the enemy. This shield covered a soldier from top to bottom, side to side and could join with others to form a wall of protection that would fend off an attacker while advancing in the field of battle.

Our faith in God protects us when the world or others tell us things are hopeless or cannot work out, because we have the One True God who is all-knowing and all-powerful. We trust in His love for us and know that He has a plan for us, to give us hope and a future with Him in eternity. Every time He keeps a promise, or delivers us from some trouble, or stands with us in hardship, it builds our faith - strengthens our shields! And when we stand beside other believers in their faith, we are protected even more! And can move against the enemy.

The **Helmet of Salvation** protects our head and identifies who we fight for. This helmet also protects our minds and helps guard our thoughts. The enemy would want to fill our minds with thoughts of doubt, fear and insecurity. But when thoughts and emotional responses are stirred up, we can hold them up to the light of truth: scripture. God's Word is the truth that will combat all that would discourage us. So we take every thought captive, and if false, replace it with God's Word.

And the **Sword of the Spirit** is God's Word, and strikes at the lies the devil would use to try and defeat us. We can use it to refute any lies the devil tries to get us to believe. We can pray it as part of our prayers. We can speak it out loud as an attack on the enemy. The enemy trembles because there is power in the Word of God.

Here is a sample prayer:

*Heavenly Father, I come before You with thanks for the armor that You give me, which is the best. With the Belt of Truth fastened around my waist, I say that I will not believe the lies the devil would try to use to confuse me. Give me clarity and understanding. Help me see past what the world and others would tell me, to what You want to say to me.*

*I place the Helmet of Salvation on my head to guard and guide my mind, and I take every thought captive to You. The Breastplate of Righteousness I put over my chest to protect my heart.*

*I wear the Shoes of the Gospel of Peace to say that I am ready to hear from You and obey what You tell me to do, and will follow where You lead. Light my path and direct me, so I know the way to go.*

*I take up my Shield of Faith to repel all the arguments and attacks the evil one sends against me. And I take up the Sword of the Sprit, the Word of God, as a weapon to help me fight and stand firm against the devil's schemes.*

*Go with me into battle, and give me victory! Amen.*

# Appendix C: Fasting

Fasting is a spiritual discipline taught in the Bible. Jesus expected His followers to fast and said that God rewards fasting. He gave us some instruction as well:

*When you fast, do not look somber like the hypocrites do, for they disfigure their faces to show men they are fasting. Truly I tell you, they have received their reward in full. But when you fast, put oil on your head and wash your face, so that it will not be obvious to others that you are fasting, but only to your Father, who is unseen; and your Father, who sees what is done in secret, will reward you.* (Matthew 6:16-18)

Often in the Bible, God's people fasted right before a major victory, miracle or answer to prayer. It prepared them to hear and receive from God. Moses fasted before receiving the 10 Commandments (Exodus 34:28); Nehemiah before he undertook a great work for God (Nehemiah 1:4); Esther and her people before she sought the favor of the king to save her people (Esther 4:15-17); early Christians at a time of decision (Acts 13:2-3). And of course, Jesus fasted.

HOWEVER, be assured that fasting is:

NOT as much about food as it is about focus;

NOT as much about saying no to the body
as it is about saying yes to the Spirit;

NOT about doing without, but about looking within.

This is something we can do to demonstrate to God the depth of our desire to submit before Him, asking Him to "clear our plate" of anything in us that is not of Him. Also in scripture, when there was holy work to be done, those involved would fast to cleanse themselves spiritually in preparation to be used by God.

Fasting means to reduce or eliminate your intake of food or a behavior for a specific time and purpose. You can use the time you'd normally spend in these activities for reading scripture and prayer. Whenever you think of food, or the activity, use it as a prompt to pray.

Your time in prayer should include all aspects of communication with our Father:

**Praise** Him for who He is. Read scripture, like Psalm 8, 33, 103 or sing some praise songs.

**Repent:** Confess your sin, turn from it and be cleansed before Him. Read Psalm 32, 51, or Isaiah 59:1-2

**Ask** for His blessing on your life, your family, your church, your community, your country, or an issue you've been dealing with.

**Yield** to His response. Pray expecting to hear answers, allowing for time to just listen.  Or read scripture to see what He has to say to you.

Are you ready to consider a fast? Some types of fasts are:

- Water fast – abstain from all food and juices

- Juice fast – only drink fruit and vegetable juices

- Partial fast – eliminate certain foods or specific meal

- Non-food fast -like watching TV, using social media or the internet, talking, or some other activity you normally spend time on.

The length of a fast can vary as well. Please be wise and evaluate your participation with your personal health needs.

Whether you eat or not, this can be a great opportunity to set aside a time to feast on the LORD to show that you are:

– willing to be humbled and molded before Him

– willing to be cleansed and set apart to do His will

– willing to sacrifice personal pleasure for time with Him

***So we fasted and prayed to God about this, and he answered our prayer.*** (Ezra 8:23)

# *Appendix D: How You Tune In to God's Voice*

I believe God is speaking to us, or sending out His signal, all the time, through His Word, His Son, His Creation, and our circumstances, among other ways. His is a constant, uninterruptible, full-strength signal. But we need to tune in to hear it.

God has built into us a receiver to hear Him. It's His spirit. We are all made up of body, mind and spirit. As a believer, we also have the Holy Spirit within us who helps us hear Him even better. And the Holy Spirit helps us understand what we hear.

His is a perfect "wireless" connection that is never out of service, out of range, broken, interrupted by weather conditions, satellite position, or earthly circumstances. But here are three reasons we may not be "tuned in."

1.  We don't know God's frequencies — here are a few:

    ***Prayer — Scripture — Nature — Circumstances***
    ***Dreams — Pain — Sermons — Bible Study***
    ***People — Podcasts — Christian books — Revelations***

    **Ask yourself:** Are you tuning in to and exposing yourself to the sources God is broadcasting on?

    - Make time for those opportunities regularly in your day, your week.
    - Ask God to speak to you in ways you will notice and understand.
    - You might try a "Tune In Exercise" (Appendix E)

2.  Like your physical ears, we can't hear clearly if the noise level around us is drowning out what God is saying. And we have inner voices we often focus on that keep us from hearing what God has to say.

    **Ask yourself:** Are you paying more attention to what you hear in the world and within yourself?

    - Invite the Holy Spirit to silence all ungodly sources and distractions.
    - Ask that confusion, preconceived ideas, biases, and misconceptions be sent away.
    - And ask the Holy Spirit to reveal truth, clarify meaning, and show application to your life.

3.  You have an "ear" infection. Spiritually, sin can block our ability to communicate effectively with God.

    **Ask yourself:** Have you cleaned out your "spiritual ears" lately?

    - Be willing to confess your sin to God and turn from it.
    - He will forgive you and that will re-establish your communication.
    - For more information, see Confession and Repentance in Appendix A.

# *Appendix E: Four Tune-In Exercises for Hearing God*

God speaks in so many different ways, I can't list them all. He is so creative and you are unique. Here are four exercises you can try that have worked for others.

Begin by asking God to speak to you in a way that you will recognize and understand. He WILL answer your prayer. Although it can happen, you may not hear an audible, physical voice.

### Exercise One

Set aside a time to get alone and just be still. Arrange for no interruptions. Turn off your cell phone or anything else that might distract you. For some people it helps to be outdoors without the distractions of the house or apartment. For others, a quiet room works.

> Start a conversation with God. You can speak out loud, or with your inner voice — He can hear you. Begin by thanking God — for who He is, for what He's done in your life or in the world. Or begin with a question you have, or share with Him something that's weighing on your heart or concerning you.

> Then quiet yourself and listen. Eyes open is ok unless that distracts you. Eyes closed works too. Ask the Holy Spirit to help you sense what God is saying. He may speak to you in words of comfort, or love, instruction or change your perspective. He may place a picture or vision in your mind. He may sing you a song or direct you to Scripture.

> Write down what you hear. Then check it against Scripture in "Hearing from God" (Appendix F) and the "Hearing from God Worksheet" (Appendix G).

### Exercise Two

Plan uninterrupted time without others nearby to observe what is around you.

> If you can go outside, are there birds, trees, flowers, clouds, mountains, water, some piece of God's creation that might have a message for you? Do you see something that shows you something about yourself, or about God? Do you see something that reflects some inner truth?

> If inside, look out a window, or at art, or the colors or items around you and check for any memories or feelings they evoke. Do you need a fresh look at an area of your life? Do you need help dealing with emotions that may have surfaced?

## *Exercise Three*

Get alone in a comfortable place where you can read or listen. Open your Bible or listen to scripture being read aloud. If you've been reading regularly, start where you left off. If not you might consider looking at the One Year Bible website and choose the scripture selection for that day. God may direct you to a place to begin. If this is new to you, start with the book of John. Or Joshua. Or 1 John.

> Start reading and read until you hear something that resonates with something you are going through. It may be a message of instruction, or encouragement, or a revelation about yourself or God. A verse may stand out with a new significance or a better understanding than it has had before. Or it may shine a light that gives you a new perspective.

> Ask what this means. And what it means to you. Is there something you need to change — to do, or stop doing, with this new understanding? Is there a warning you need to heed? An example for you to follow? Is God showing you something about Himself? About yourself in these verses?

## *Exercise Four*

Freestyle: Talk to God Wherever you are, whenever — day or night, whatever the circumstances. You can say anything to Him. Whisper your fears, yell your frustrations, rage against your circumstances. He can take it all. Pour out your heart about what you are facing. Ask for His perspective. Or for clarification on an issue.

> Are you experiencing blessing? Confusion? Pain? What in your circumstances is speaking the loudest? Ask God to show you where He is in that circumstance and ask Him for wisdom to cope with it. What you can learn from it. How can you share the blessing? What can you learn from your pain? Who can you connect with because of your blessing, confusion or pain?

> Then pause to hear His answer. Do you need a change of attitude? A course correction? Do you hear a word of encouragement? Direction? Or feel a sense of comfort?

> Can you comfort, direct or encourage someone else with what you hear?

# Appendix F: Hearing from God

> **Now then, my children, listen to me;**
> **blessed are those who keep my ways.**
> **Listen to my instruction and be wise;**
> **do not disregard it.**
> **Blessed are those who listen to me,**
> **watching daily at my doors,**
> **waiting at my doorway.**
> **For those who find me find life**
> **and receive favor from the Lord.**
>
> **Proverbs 8:32–5**

## How do I know if what I hear is from God or some other voice?

When you believe you've heard from God You, write it down and put it to the test. Ask these three questions to see if you heard it from God or some other source:

### 1. Does what I hear agree with the Bible?

**The answer must be "yes."** God will never tell you anything that contradicts what He has already said in His Word. So, spend time in and be familiar with the Bible.

If you need help, a Christian friend or pastor can help you find scriptures dealing with your topic. If there is nothing, or you are unsure, ask God to reveal the truth to you.

One role of the Holy Spirit who dwells in every believer is to teach us, guiding us in truth. In John 14:26, Jesus tells us the Holy Spirit will teach us all things. And in John 16:13 tells us the Holy Spirit will guide us into all truth.

### 2. Will the result, or the fruit of the act, be the fruit of the Spirit?

**This answer should also be "yes."** The result of what you hear should lead to and produce the fruit of the Spirit in your life and those around you.

Galatians 5:22-23 outlines the fruit of the Spirit as: love, joy, peace, patience, kindness, goodness, faithfulness, gentleness, and self-control.

Verses 19-21 tell us the acts of the flesh are immorality, impurity, debauchery, idolatry, witchcraft, hatred, discord, jealousy, rage, selfish ambition, dissension, envy, and the like.

So if you act on what you think God is telling you, what will happen? Look at the expected result, or the "fruit," to see where it leads.

**3. Will it benefit my relationship with God?**

**Again, this answer should be "yes."** Everything you do will either benefit or weaken your relationship with God.

Micah 6:8,
> *...And what does the Lord require of you?*
> *To act justly and to love mercy*
> *and to walk humbly with your God.*

Most of the time, the Holy Spirit will tell you if what you are doing is pulling you away from God. You will probably be able to sense that you are either drawing closer to God or pulling away if you were to follow through on what you think you hear Him telling you.

It might help to ask another Christian friend, pastor or counselor. Or even pose the question: What Would Jesus do?

**If you hit a "no," stop right there!** What you heard is NOT from God. If it

— **does NOT agree with the Bible, or**

— **does NOT produce the Fruit of the Spirit, or**

— **does NOT benefit your relationship with God,**

**then it is NOT from God.**

## So what do I do?

**1. If you got a NO** to *any* of the three questions:

Pray for strength to say "no" to that and keep seeking God's wisdom.

James 1:5 says "If any of you lacks wisdom, you should ask God, who gives generously to all without finding fault, and it will be given to you." So ask again for God's input.

**2. If you got a YES** to *all* three questions:

Pray for the strength and courage to follow through on what God has shown you.

Paul encourages us that we can do all things through Christ who strengthens us. (Philippians 4:13)

If confusion still exists, go back and ask God for clarity. And be patient. The answer may be unclear because the timing isn't right. Be willing to wait on God's timing.

Psalm 27:14, **Wait for the Lord; be strong and take heart and wait for the Lord.**

# Appendix G: Hearing from God Worksheet

## Is what I'm hearing from God?

*If any of you lacks wisdom, you should ask God, who gives generously to all without finding fault, and it will be given to you.*

**James 1:5**

If you hit a "no," stop there.  Is it NOT from God.

What is my concern or question?

_______________________________________________

_______________________________________________

What am I hearing?

_______________________________________________

_______________________________________________

What does the Bible say about my concern and what I am hearing?

_______________________________________________

_______________________________________________

_______________________________________________

Does what I am hearing agree with the Bible?        **YES ☐  NO ☐**

If I act on what I've heard, what will it produce in my life and others?

_______________________________________________

_______________________________________________

_______________________________________________

Is that a Fruit of the Spirit?        **YES ☐  NO ☐**

If I act on what I've heard, will it benefit my relationship with God?   **YES ☐  NO ☐**

# Appendix H: Guide to Salvation Prayer

So the person you've been praying for has suddenly called you up, dropped all pretense, and is now asking you what they need to do next. They're ready to surrender their life to Christ.

Sweet! You've done all the hard work, praying for them each day. This next part is simplicity itself: ***Accept, Believe, Confess.***

You **accept** that Jesus is who He says He is in the Bible — the Son of God. And **believe** that His sacrifice and death on the cross paid the penalty for your sin, and that God raised Him from the dead. **Confess** that you need His help to acknowledge your sin, and turn from how you've been living and instead choose to follow Him in this life each and every day from now on. That's pretty much it.

Ask Him to come into your life, wipe out the sin that separates you from God, and then thank Him for making it all happen. Done. Now celebrate!

Rather have the "read through" version you're now used to? No problem. Read and pray this together and you're all set, except for the celebration hugs.

> *Father, it is written in Your Word that if I confess with my mouth that Jesus is Lord and believe in my heart that You have raised Him from the dead, I shall be saved.*
>
> *Therefore, Father, I confess that Jesus is my Lord. I make Him Lord of my life right now. I believe in my heart that You raised Jesus from the dead. I turn from my past life and decisions, accepting Your payment for my sin, and choose to follow You from now on.*
>
> *I thank You for forgiving me of all my sin and making me a new creation! Old things have passed away; now all things become new in Jesus' name. Amen.*

# *Appendix I: Who You Are in Christ*

What happens the split second after you choose to trust in God?

When you choose to become a believer in Jesus Christ, you are changed in ways you and I cannot imagine. In an instant, who you are and what's true of you have all completely changed.

Take time to review the list of just some of these changes below.

I am chosen of God, holy and dearly loved. Colossians 3:12

I am chosen and dearly loved by Christ to bear his fruit. John 15:16

I am the salt of the earth. Matthew 5:13

I am a child of God. John 1:12

I am a daughter/son of light and not darkness. I Thessalonians 5:5

I have been made righteous. 2 Corinthians 5:21

I am free forever from condemnation. Romans 8:1

I am united to the LORD and am one spirit with him. I Corinthians 6:17

I am a member of Christ's body. I Cor 12:27, Ephesians 5:30

I am a holy partaker of a heavenly calling. Hebrews 3:1

I have been redeemed and forgiven, and I am the recipient of his lavish grace. I have been made alive together with Christ. Ephesians 2:5

I may approach God with boldness, freedom and confidence. Ephesians 3:12

I have been redeemed and forgiven of all my sins. The debt against me has been cancelled. Colossians 1:14

Christ Himself is in me. Colossians 1:27

I have been made complete in Christ. Colossians 2:10

I have been given the spirit of power, love and a sound mind. 2 Timothy 1:7

I am God's handiwork, created in Christ Jesus to do the work which He has prepared in advance for me. Ephesians 2:10

I am born of God, and the evil one, the devil, cannot touch me. 1 John 5:18

There will be a lot of voices speaking into your new way of life. Old friends, new friends, family members and more. Even your own internal "negative self-talk" might start to sound different to you now.

Did any of the truths above sound similar to something you've "heard" is *not* true of you? From your friends? Inside your own head, maybe? Saying — it couldn't possibly be true of you. No way — and yet? Maybe take a moment to review those specific truth claims again.

Even better, write out those verses on sticky notes and put them in places where you will be sure to see each one in the coming days, weeks and months. You're running a race now, and you don't want to get distracted by conflicting opinions and veer out of your lane.

Your life in Christ is just beginning. The evil one is not pleased, but that's just too bad. You belong to Christ now, and everything is about to get amazing!

***But you are a chosen people, a royal priesthood, a holy nation, God's special possession, that you may declare the praises of him who called you out of darkness into his wonderful light.*** (1 Peter 2:9)

# Appendix J : Forgiving Others

Life happens. People let us down, or betray us. Sometimes by accident. Sometimes intentionally, and with malice.

So if something has happened that caused you pain — physical, psychological, mental, or emotional — or someone has hurt your feelings or enraged you, you may find it hard to forgive others, yourself, or even God.

Unforgiveness can cause a bitterness in our spirit, and actually keeps negative emotions and attitudes in the forefront of our minds. It can harden our hearts or make us feel angry or sad all the time or like victims. None of that is good for our physical, mental or spiritual health.

> *It's been said that unforgiveness is like drinking poison and expecting the other person to get sick or die. Or like being a prisoner to the negative emotions and permanent upset from the offense, while the perpetrator walks free!*

Don't let unforgiveness make you sick, bitter, and unhappy. Don't allow those past events to keep you chained to the offense and focused on vengeance. Instead, learn to walk in the freedom of forgiveness!

The truth is, you will be doubly blessed when you forgive.

1. You are being obedient because God commands us to forgive.

2. You set yourself free from the negative emotions and attitudes that cause foul moods, anger and bitterness.

Here are some truths about Forgiveness:

- Forgiveness doesn't mean you approve of or condone what was done or said. Or that you're even ok with it.

- Forgiveness doesn't mean you will necessarily forget. Many times, it is wise for you to remember in order to learn from the hurt to protect yourself.

- Forgiveness doesn't mean the offender is free from consequences or from God's judgement.

- Forgiveness doesn't mean you have to renew or have an ongoing relationship with the other person. It may not even be wise to try.

- Forgiveness may often come with new boundaries or restrictions on acceptable circumstances or behaviors in relationships that will protect you from being hurt again.

- Sometimes forgiveness comes in stages. You may feel you've forgiven someone, and then a new wave of upset and anger or sadness comes over you. Or as time passes, you discover an impact the offense has on your life or the lives of your loved ones that is just presenting itself. Do the work again, asking God to lead you to a new level of forgiveness.

Sometimes you may need to forgive someone who's no longer alive, or who lives far away. Or it may not be smart to even have contact with the person you need to forgive. Just getting right with yourself and God about the situation may be what you need. God can change your heart, your attitude. And heal you from the harm caused without contact with the other person.

- This can happen through a time set aside for you and God to meet in prayer. He can lead you in what to do. Sometimes writing a letter you do not send, is beneficial. Sometimes it's having a pretend conversation, imaging you are speaking to the offender, sharing your perspective on the hurt that's been caused.

- Other times, talking with a Christian pastor or counselor is greatly beneficial.

Let God show you how to arrive at the place where you can forgive and let go of the bitterness and hurt. And trust God with justice.

A good resource is Charles Stanley's book *The Gift of Forgiveness* (Nashville: Thomas Nelson, 2002), available at most online retailers, bookstores and libraries.

# Appendix K: Spiritual Protection Scripture Prayer

Ephesians 6:12, **For our struggle is not against flesh and blood, but against the rulers, against the authorities, against the powers of this dark world and against the spiritual forces of evil in the heavenly realms.**

Heavenly Father, protect and guide _____'s comings and goings. Do not let _____ seek or be drawn away by the temporary pleasures of evil. Help them see evil for what it is.

You tell us there are spiritual enemies who seek to undermine _____'s faith and ability to do the work You created them to do. So I put _____'s name into Psalm 35 and pray Your words against every ruler, authority and power of this dark world, and the spiritual forces in the heavenly realms who set themselves against You and Your will for _____, in order to protect their life, health, family, relationships, home, school or work, finances, mental and emotional well-being and spiritual growth.

**Psalm 35 Of David.**

1   *Contend, Lord, with those who contend with [_____];*
        *fight against those who fight against [them].*

2   *Take up shield and armor;*
        *arise and come to [their] aid.*

3   *Brandish spear and javelin*
        *against those who pursue [_____].*
    *Say to [_____],*
        *"I am your salvation."*

4   *May those who seek [_____'s] life*
        *be disgraced and put to shame;*
    *may those who plot [_____'s] ruin*
        *be turned back in dismay.*

5   *May they be like chaff before the wind,*
        *with the angel of the Lord driving them away;*

6   *may their path be dark and slippery,*
        *with the angel of the Lord pursuing them.*

7   *Since they hid their net for [_____] without cause*
        *and without cause dug a pit for [them],*

8   *may ruin overtake them by surprise —*
        *may the net they hid entangle them,*
        *may they fall into the pit, to their ruin.*

9   Then my soul will rejoice in the Lord
        and delight in his salvation.

10 My whole being will exclaim,
        "Who is like you, Lord?

. . . . . . . . . . . . . . . . . . . . . . .

17 How long, Lord, will you look on?
        Rescue [_____] from their ravages,
        [their] precious life from these lions.

18 I will give you thanks in the great assembly;
        among the throngs I will praise you.

19 Do not let those gloat over [_____]
        who are [their] enemies without cause;
    do not let those who hate [_____] without reason
        maliciously wink the eye.

20 They do not speak peaceably,
        but devise false accusations
        against those who live quietly in the land.

21 They sneer at [_____] and say, "Aha! Aha!
        With our own eyes we have seen it."

22 Lord, you have seen this; do not be silent.
        Do not be far from [_____], Lord.

23 Awake, and rise to [_____'s] defense!
        Contend for [them], my God and Lord.

24 Vindicate [_____] in your righteousness, Lord my God;
        do not let them gloat over [_____].

25 Do not let them think, "Aha, just what we wanted!"
        or say, "We have swallowed [them] up."

26 May all who gloat over [_____'s] distress
        be put to shame and confusion;
    may all who exalt themselves over [_____]
        be clothed with shame and disgrace.

27 May those who delight in [_____'s] vindication
        shout for joy and gladness;
    may they always say, "The Lord be exalted,
        who delights in the well-being of his servant."

28 My tongue will proclaim Your righteousness,
        Your praises all day long.

# Appendix L: List of Images by Day

Cover — Co-author and a Tree, looking towards home...

Acknowledgments — The stormy Front Range of Colorado

Introduction to the 40-Day Guides — Narrow, once muddy slot canyon, Grand Staircase/Escalante, UT

Song lyrics — Steamy hot spring, south of Las Vegas, NV

Day 1 — Confederate Soldier re-enactor, Old Fort Jackson, Savannah, GA

Day 2 — Cliff Dancing, Moab, UT

Day 3 — Bible in use, Colorado Springs, CO

Day 4 — Seagull enjoying a sunset flight, Gulf Shores, AL

Day 5 — co-Author being goofy, Travertine Canyon, during a Grand Canyon float trip

Day 6 — End of season aspen tree, near Blue Mesa Reservoir, Gunnison, CO

Day 7 — Paraglider at sunrise, Corona Arch, outside Moab, UT

Day 8 — Breaktime, rock climbers on Montezuma's Tower, Garden of the Gods, Colorado Springs, CO

Day 9 — American alligator, near Silver Springs, FL

Day 10 — Glacier Lake, Montana backcountry

Day 11 — perturbed little finch, somewhere in Louisiana

Day 12 — Stemming, entrance to slot canyon, outside Zion National Park, UT

Day 13 — Twisty creek just below Dallas Divide, CO

Day 14 — Lightning strike, Cheyenne Mountain and the Garden, Colorado Springs, CO

Day 15 — Dreamy waterfall, Rainbow Springs park, FL

Day 16 — Narrow squeeze, Utah backcountry

Day 17 — Crossing Gore Creek, the vertical way. Vail, CO

Day 18 — Quiet pier, Gulf coast, FL

Day 19 — Sunset views, driving near Jacksonville, FL

Day 20 — Thrilled hiker, turned model at Linville Falls, Linville Gorge, NC

Day 21 — Mountaintop, near Canon City, CO

Halfway Point Check — Photo Op, "Windows" section of Arches National Park, UT

*Day 22 — Forgotten pier, Lake Pontchartrain, LA*

*Day 23 — Navigating "Boy Scout Canyon," a slot canyon near Hoover Dam*

*Day 24 — Paddle hard and hang on! Smashing a wave, Arkansas River, CO*

*Day 25 — High meadow above Telluride, CO*

*Day 26 — Cliff jumping, Westwater Canyon float trip on the Colorado River, UT*

*Day 27 — Glorious aspen trees, Lost Creek Wilderness Area, near Tarryall, CO*

*Day 28 — Mesmerizing surf, Atlantic coast near Cape Canaveral, FL*

*Day 29 — Lower Calf Creek Falls hike, near Escalante, UT*

*Day 30 — Crooked Island Beach, Tyndall Air Force Base, Panama City, FL*

*Day 31 — Locals hanging out, Shingle Creek, Kissimmee, FL*

*Day 32 — Narrow rappel, slot canyon, Zion National Park, UT*

*Day 33 — Indian Creek climbing area, near Moab, UT*

*Day 34 — Black Canyon of the Gunnison National Park, near Montrose, CO*

*Day 35 — Group hike at The Crags, west side of Pikes Peak, near Divide, CO*

*Day 36 — Tough rockfall to negotiate, Goldstrike Canyon, near Hoover Dam*

*Day 37 — Getting ready for my turn on rappel. Canyoneering, Utah wilderness*

*Day 38 — Sunset on a grassy hillside, Parkdale, CO*

*Day 39 — Mountaintop, Blue Ridge Parkway, NC*

*Day 40 — Silver Lining, and then some, Colorado high country*

*Priestly Blessing — Pedestrian Bridge, Colorado River outside Moab, UT*

*Thank You After 40 Days — Backpacking through Eagles Nest wilderness Area, near Breckenridge, CO*

*Appendices — Crimson fountain grass, catching late day sunshine, Dallas, TX*


*Interlude and Reflection images (in no order)*

*Waterfall, Starved Rock State Park, IL*

## About the Authors

### Eric Sprinkle

A former Whitewater Guide and Swift-water Rescue Instructor for the U.S. military, Eric travels the country speaking about the benefits of risk, managing fear, and how to make life more exciting by "living a slightly more dangerous lifestyle." He calls the multi-sport playground of Colorado Springs home. He's also managed to get lost on mountain tops, in river canyons and busy shopping malls, so he totally understands how wandering happens. But also, how God continues to be faithful.

Find more about him at AdventureExperience.net, including Speaker info, free book images, and an action-packed YouTube channel full of waterfalls, cliff faces, and whitewater silliness.

### Laura Shaffer

An Army Brat moving almost every year till college, Laura was delighted to discover that wherever she went, God was always there ahead of her. Houses, schools and friends changed, but there was always Church or Chapel where she learned, and felt, that God was with her.

God is there for our Wayward Believers too. Whatever place they're in God will provide people, circumstances and more ways than we can even think of to reach and draw our loved ones back to Him. Being intentional and consistent in prayer not only deepens our own relationship with the Lord, but releases showers of blessing that grow miracles in our lives and those we pray for. She hopes this book will do that for you.

Check out Laura's blogs: www.DailyBiblePrayer.wordpress.com for Scripture-based prayers anytime, and her inspirational writings at www.HearMoreFromGod.wordpress.com

# LOVE LAURA'S

## PRAYERS?

Looking for more from your new prayer partner Laura?

You've got it!

Have a look here for daily prayers, inspiring blogs, and more!

Check out her prayer blog—
www.dailyBibleprayer.wordpress.com
For her devotion blog—
www.hearmorefromGod.wordpress.com

## Additional Thoughts on Praying
for Your Wayward Loved One

Need someone to talk about
- Risk and Challenge
- Making your life more Exciting
- Dealing better with Fear

Eric would love to hang out with your group!

He's ready to unpack the question of whether our Lord God calls us to adventure, and even share some fun stories about prayer books too! All with heart pounding stories and gorgeous photos!

Check out AdventureExperience.net today and let's connect for an inspiring, challenging time together!

# Additional Thoughts on Praying for Your Wayward Loved One

# More from Adventure Experience Press

### Adventure Devos:

The first devotional written exclusively for men with a heart for Risk and Danger

### Adventure Devos: Women's Edition:

An exciting devotional written exclusively for women with a Heart for Risk and Adventure

### Adventure Devos: Youth Edition:

Summer Camp never has to end when your devotional takes you adventuring all year long!

*"Adventure Devos will challenge any man to be a better father or husband in no time, no doubt about it. Just read a few of the book's 'Dares' and see for yourself how easily this devotional will get anyone into applying God's Word."*
Megan "Katniss" Autrey, Colorado Certified Whitewater Guide Instructor, Wife and Mother

# Additional Thoughts on Praying for Your Wayward Loved One

# Additional Thoughts on Praying
for Your Wayward Loved One

www.ingramcontent.com/pod-product-compliance
Lightning Source LLC
Chambersburg PA
CBHW061732050726
47598CB00002B/453